A DANGEROUS RECIPE

A DANGEROUS RECIPE

GEE SVASTI

RIVER BOOKS

First published and distributed in 2018 by
River Books
396 Maharaj Road, Tatien, Bangkok 10200
Tel. 66 2 622-1900, 224-6686
Fax. 66 2 225-3861
E-mail: order@riverbooksbk.com
www.riverbooksbk.com

Editor: Narisa Chakrabongse
Production supervision: Paisarn Piemmettawat
Design: Ruetairat Nanta

ISBN 978 616 7339 82 5

Printed and bound in Thailand by UPadd International Co., Ltd.

Gee Svasti, born in the UK to a Thai mother
and an English father, has worked in television,
design and technology. Founder of several successful
companies in publishing and new media,
he currently lives between London and Bangkok.
A Dangerous Recipe is his first novel.

Prelude

What's the secret to taste?

Why do some meal's trigger elation, while others return only indifference even disgust? And that rift between love and loathing, no more than a handful of molecules in between.

Science has standard explanations. Taste buds on our tongues, each containing up to a dozen receptor cells, send messages through nerve channels to the brain; this is salty, this is bitter, this is sour; this is going to kill me. Other senses, of smell, texture and feel, come into play; a composite picture of gourmet delight or cheap corner store chicken.

What confounds this mechanistic view is the fact that our taste cells are continually dying and being replaced. The structure changes yet our proclivities and frailties remain.

Within the mind such mysteries only deepen. Shapes can influence taste; chocolates that are round are perceived to be sweeter; triangular shapes deemed to be bitter. Colours also dramatically affect our reaction to flavour; vivacity of hue signalling potency and intensity. External factors are just as persuasive. Positive music lifts our moods and expectations, sombre tones repress a sense of contentment. And few of us can deny having heightened reactions to a meal purely on the basis of price.

And then there is memory. The merest hint of an ingredient can recall scenes from the past; the smell of over boiled cabbage and floor cleaner rekindle an image of a long forgotten school corridor. Marcel Proust's now famous madeleine moment, although the author's earlier drafts described the effect of more mundane toast and honey, might genuinely reflect a lust for Aunt Léonie's unrivalled bakery skills, but the bond also unlocked more profound associations; his nostalgia for his Combray childhood, the comfort of the family home, the scent of wild roses from the walled garden.

Words can often be enough to prompt such heightened states. The mere mention of 'home' projecting the sensation of fresh scones, cream and jam; 'football', the sweet, refreshing allure of sliced oranges at half time.

The food industry, with its scientists, designers, molecular mixologists and manufacturers, has leveraged the powers of psychology to entice us with more. A walk down a local supermarket aisle will shower us with more choice and variety than our grandparents had in a lifetime. Our desire for novelty; new tastes, new flavours, has warped into overdrive. Peruvian quinoa, Madagascan baobab, and Nordic lingonberries join the thousands of novel ingredients that flow through our fryers, grill pans, pressure steamers and skillets.

As evidenced by the words of the 19th century writer and professor of gastronomy, Jean Anthelme Brillat-Savarin, in *The Philosopher in the Kitchen*, "The discovery of a new dish does more for human happiness than the discovery of a star."

One

The Hiro San Inn had been difficult to find. Perched on the end of an old weatherbeaten pier at the edge of the old fishing port, very few had made the arduous journey through the winding and often damp market side streets. For the tech savvy there was no marker in Google maps, no website online, not even a land line for reservations. And at journey's end there was likely to be disappointment. It was small. There were only five mean and uncomfortable tables. But Hiro San's notoriety, like a secret cipher passed only amongst a select few, ensured that those tables were always filled.

Despite being the last week of October the evening was warm enough for those five tables to be outside. Local shop owners and older residents, only too aware of the rush for places, came early. By seven o'clock two of the larger tables were already full. Cold namizake Saki, served in raw, earthenware cups, was shared between the two groups. Although most of these diners knew each other, their conversation, usually animated, was on this particular evening, subdued.

There had been rumours. In the low rise streets of Shitomae, land surveyors with laser scanners and optical theodolites had been spotted. A week before two mini buses had parked up at the entrance of the former ferry terminal. A line of dark-suited executives had descended. Dragging along with them a small retinue of construction engineers, urban planners and architects, they had walked along the narrow promenade in the face of a howling gale, clip boards held up like shields against the salty spray from the waves. At the far end of the port they had been picked up by the same silver Mercedes vans and rushed back to the warmth of the city.

Speculation was rife that a large property development was being planned. Threatening many of the older arcades, this high rise residential complex would see most of the traditional Dozo storehouses (characterised by their thick timber frames and soot black plaster walls), pulled down.

The plans were dividing the community. To add to the controversy, several established families in the area had already succumbed to the generous deals on offer and sold up. It was clear to anyone with even the most rudimentary map that the location of the two-hundred-year-old restaurant at the end of the pier was the critical key to unlocking the 'wealth' of the site. But the developers had come up against a formidable obstacle. The current owner, the seventy-one-year-old chef, Mori Takeshi, was the immovable rock that blocked their ambitions. For two months a trail of executives had beat a path to his door. Subtle gifts and noble sentiments had descended to vulgar inducements then crude threats. Nothing had worked. Baffled by his rejection, they had come away infuriated by the vagaries of human obstinacy; selfish narcissism they claimed.

It was said that Mori's family came from a long line of market traders. Never rich, they had run food stalls along the quayside before opening the inn. Attuned only to the needs of his immediate team within the four fragile walls of his kitchen, Mori was pathologically distrustful of all big business. His well-known house edicts were designed to discourage this grubby, grasping elite. The first concerned dress code. Anyone wearing a suit, polished shoes, even a tie, was barred from entering. His second was a behavioural warning. In the style of an old Edo woodblock, a prominent sign nailed to the entrance arch, featured a laptop and a smart phone being shattered with a meat cleaver.

Mori's final edict concerned pricing policy. If you were local and ate modestly, you were asked to pay what you thought was fair or could reasonably afford. For those suspected of being corporate stooges, bankers, or investors, the inverse was true – the restaurant charged what it thought was fair; an arbitrary judgement based on appearances, often open to the moody caprice of the owner, that could see the price of a meal skyrocket by more than three hundred percent: a sanction against the wealthy.

But word got out. For the ever-calculating minds of devious investors and hedge-fund analysts, who flaunted rules and regulations by habit, Mori's draconian edicts became just another set of challenges they had to 'reconceptualize' and overcome. Ditching their suits and Rolex watches at the office, they dressed down, parking their shiny German cars at the ferry terminal. The three block walk to the restaurant provided the time and distance to scuff their newly-bought trainers. Some, getting theatrical, had even constructed elaborate second lives – dental hygienist, *mochi*-maker, deep-sea diving instructor.

For Mori's already overworked staff this made the implementation of their special tariff hard to enforce. Several embarrassing mistakes had been made. Innocent locals, wrongly taken for bankers, had found themselves charged the full affluence tax. Conversely, some of the wealthiest executives, having rummaged through the darkest recesses of their walk-in-wardrobes to find that genuine 'second-hand' look, gleefully boasted of securing the 'pauper's' discount.

On this particular evening, two such tables aroused the suspicions of the serving staff. The first was filled with four middle-aged men, all silver haired, tanned and a touch overweight. Like everyone they had dressed casually. Yet small details betrayed; their worn and ripped jeans and shirts were ironed with a care and precision that could only mean professional staff. Mori himself had already damned the ensemble with a large 'X' against their bill. Not that they cared. With food already on the table and excited by the authenticity and raw ambience of the place, they were more than happy to pay several multiples more: marketing executives.

A third table was taken by a younger couple, Corran Brook and Jade Cheng. Corran, an Australian in his mid thirties, had a rugged and tousled look, but only because he'd just slept off a long lunch. As a foreigner he automatically qualified for the higher tax band. Yet his clothes – loose linen jacket, T-shirt and mid-grey trousers – were, for Mori's ever calculating staff, frustratingly difficult to value or define. In contrast, his partner, Jade, making no attempt to tone down her looks to pander to the rules, appeared to wilfully scorn the conventions. Slender with jet black hair, every element of her perfectly contoured dress, sculpted heels and matching jewellery provocatively screamed haute couture. Across a dining area dotted with fakes and phoneys, her brash, gratuitous looks were the subject of most of the table gossip; the girl was intentionally courting the highest surcharge – a shameless attempt at the record? Maybe not so unexpected from a member of Tokyo's more showy elite.

Corran had met Jade at a gallery opening in Shinjuku. Formerly a red-light district in the 1980's, it had been cleaned up by the government and slowly filled up with quirky retro bars, tattoo shops and hidden recording studios beloved by young hipsters courting the sub-culture. Although visibly independently wealthy, Jade had introduced herself as a web entrepreneur. She owned a media company. One of her online ventures was a YouTube food channel, "Krashkitchen"; ostensively 'how to' clips on popular Japanese cuisine. There were the obvious favourites: from basic sushi skills, to preparing *ramen* noodles, meat *teriyaki* and vegetarian *sukiyaki*. After the art show, when Corran had returned to his hotel room, he had checked out the site and scanned through some of the most viewed videos. Though the setting looked authentic – bamboo and paper screens, brush stroke calligraphy and carbonised cast-iron woks – there was also something strangely fetishistic about the cuisine. Nothing was overtly sexual. No one took their clothes off. But there was a darker side, a second meaning encoded in gestures, eye movements and the nuance of words, which to a foreigner like Corran remained baffling. The numbers for the site-four million views for even the most basic cooking skills-suggested that the fans weren't just infatuated with the presenter's kitchen talents. Corran, not wanting to be disparaging, hadn't looked further.

Drawn to the same rare dining locations, it wasn't long before their paths crossed again. At his second meeting with Jade, Corran had mentioned the almost legendary rumours swirling around the little known inn, the Hiro San. He had seen a blog post on the restaurant by a traveller who freelanced for American travel magazines. Although the piece had edged towards the verbose (more than fifteen descriptors in a single sentence), the writer had hinted at the existence of a hidden knowledge that resided at the heart of the Hiro San kitchens; a culinary secret revealed only to the immediate sons of the Takeshi clan. Mori was of the sixth generation. Perversely it was the seventy-year-old chef himself who was partly responsible for letting this enigmatic narrative escape into the modern world. At drunken moments he had been known to boast about this mysterious past; his origin myth claimed the first enlightened insight from a wandering zen sage.

The heart of the inn's reputation rested on three key dishes: scallop seaweed with *Wasabia japonica*, Wagyu beef *gyoza* and fish *tosazu*. Corran and Jade had ordered all of them. Two had already been scraped clean. To Corran's calculating mind, the flavours had come thick and fast. Ticking off the ingredients one by one in his head, it had been easy to unravel their method. But it was the third dish, the fish *tosazu*, that now preoccupied his attention; and had done for the last twenty minutes.

The heart of the dish was obvious. It was fish. In fact, bream. And it was neither expensive nor highly sought after. Indeed, it was so plentiful he had seen baskets of it selling in the fish market in Melbourne for less than $25. And that's how it appeared; plain, ordinary, cheap, served on an unglazed, white ceramic plate. Without adornment or apparent artifice, it appeared as elemental as a child's crayon sketch; rounded fins, floppy tail, fishy body. But in Corran's eyes, this lack of craft was all cruel deception: His first mouthful left him stunned. As he slowly absorbed the flavours, a rush of tastes came to the fore. There were the obvious – soy, taro paste, sweet vinegar, mirin. But infused within these known ingredients there was a subtlety that confounded him. A second mouthful revealed further hidden artistry. What Corran had taken for flakes of fish weren't even pieces of bream. They were separate layers of flesh – sometimes of prawn, crab, cuttlefish, lobster – infused with *yuzu* and *kinome* and recombined into the body of the bream with the anatomical skills of a brain surgeon. When he cut through these sections, it bled; its lifeblood an infusion of sweet umeboshi plums, raspberries and lime. These constituents might have been diverse, yet locking them together remained a single, compelling note of unusual complexity. A taste so unorthodox and allusive, that despite years of professional cooking he had failed to decipher its make up.

Japanese cuisine was all about technical mastery, dedication (measured in lifetimes rather than years) and an obsessive quest for natural and pure ingredients. Recipe books worldwide were filled with the wisdom of *shokunin*, each with their own almost 'sacred' combinations; subtle acts of preparation, seasoning, the blending of herbs and spices, their critical difference. Here sat such an infuriating conundrum; something rare, unusual, hard to pin down.

Absentmindedly Corran had trailed his fork through the layers of dark and light sauces as if attempting to unearth the answer. It left twisted waves that resembled the tortured struggles of an Edvard Munch painting.

Seconds later Corran folded his cutlery to the periphery of the dish and gave up. He wasn't enjoying the meal anymore; he'd got nowhere. His initial delight had spurred inquisitiveness, a thrill for the quest. Now with every avenue of enquiry exhausted, there was only irritation. It was as if Mori himself had deliberately served up a riddle purely to frustrate him.

Corran thought through his options. Although it was fruitless trying to reverse engineer the recipe, there were some obvious places to start. The most likely contenders were the soy (probably home made) and the *tare* – he'd heard talk of some unusual dipping potions. But to expose such a mix he was going to have to get closer to the source. And that source was at the end of a thin wooden corridor towards the back of the shack. A more devious approach was needed. He looked up from his dish and turned to Jade.

"Can you do something for me?", he interrupted.

He'd cut into a particularly sensitive episode in her narrative: her mother, on an overnight stop in Palermo before setting off on a cruise of the Aeolian Islands, had been mugged by a scooter gang. The old woman, already frail with digestive disorders, had spent the past week in a Sicilian hospital. With injuries to the side of her face and deep cuts in her shoulder (she had been dragged down a cobbled street behind the whining Piaggio, before surrendering her backpack), the sad tale should have elicited some sympathy from Corran. His sudden interjection had revealed more than insensitivity – he hadn't even been listening. Taken aback, she looked offended.

"What do you mean?" she replied, her smile uncertain.

He shrugged, "I need your help."

"Like how?"

"I want you to do something random, cause a scene."

Jade looked uncomfortable. "What kind of 'scene'?"

Corran checked behind him. He was aware his request might seem strange – "I don't know, smash a glass, fall over, break a light, that kind of thing".

"What for, Corran? Some kind of game?"

"It's no game Jade, I'm serious."

"What for?" she snapped back.

"Because I need something. And for that I need to get into the kitchen."

"Why?"

"That's my problem."

Jade looked dismayed. This wasn't the evening she had looked forward to. His distractedness, lack of intimacy and an almost fanatical focus on the food (he'd even squeezed greasy squid tentacles between his fingers to gauge its texture) had been painful enough. And now this, a crazy request out of the blue. What could he want, what was he after? His furtive glances left and right, like a thief casing a joint, further unsettled her. Nervously fingering the crystals of her necklace, she felt dejected. Her mind flicked through the set of evenings that might have been. She'd had ambitious plans; a media project she wanted to pass by him – and if that had gone well, even thoughts of passion; a forlorn wish now hopelessly crushed.

Jade glanced back across the table, hoping Corran would break a smile, show that he was just joking, messing with her. But he was unflinching, even a touch nervous: he meant it.

"Like this?" she hissed, raising her arm and knocking her glass over the table.

The wine, flowing over the rough table top, quickly spilled onto his lap. Corran, wiping the stain, remained unimpressed.

"Too tame, way too tame," he whispered.

Jade reached across for her water. Holding the glass by the stem, she flicked the cold mineral water in an arc across his face.

Corran, again unmoved, calmly wiped the cool liquid from his forehead. "Better," he replied, "but still not enough."

"What then?" she flared.

Corran leant closer, "I want you to do something that will get everyone's attention. Something big, something loud, some kind of disturbance that will distract all the staff. I need at least sixty seconds."

"You're mad Corran. Crazy. There's no way I'm doing it."

Corran calmly got up from the table. As he turned for the passageway he could sense her silently mouthing obscenities behind his back. She said she wouldn't do it. He knew she would.

Mori Takeshi worked with only a handful of staff. Most were close family ensuring both their loyalty and integrity. Unlike conventional restaurants that relied on a head chef with sous chefs and a team of underlings, Mori arranged it so that a single cook was master of each table. So there were five. A circle of dishes surrounded a central work station. With vegetables, mushrooms and meats selected and arranged in wicker baskets and ceramic bowls, they sliced and prepared the ingredients, applied the essential spices, then cooked it all above modest charcoal burners. The real artistry was at the end of the line. Mori alone commanded the sauces. His was the master craft, the final magic, the grand finale that people travelled from miles around to savour.

The unexpected violence of the noise on the veranda took everyone by surprise. The deafening 'boom' shook the old oak frame of the building, rattling the pots and pans that hung from hooks on the wall of the kitchen. Even Corran, well aware of Jade's graceful but unathletic build, was shaken. It sounded like a fight, as if a table had been upended and thrown to the floor. Those who had been at the restaurant long enough recalled a past incident when a typhoon had torn a trawler from its anchorage and it had drifted across the harbour mouth before colliding into the landing stage. Thinking it was a similar accident, the cooks all abandoned their cooking and immediately headed for the door. Even Mori, ever tied to his sacred work station, instinctively followed. The last two to leave passed Corran hidden in the shadows of the corridor. He waited a beat to check there was no one left inside, then parting the pleated curtain that hung over the opening, entered.

Though Corran had heard tales about the Hiro San's notorious antiquity, the kitchen at the back of the dining area was still a bit of a shock. Clumsy, earthenware vessels resting on crude stone plinths warmed by wooden burners, were so scarred and blackened by soot they looked medieval. Old oak boards, black with age, must have been original. Worn, polished indentations between the tables and work stations, betrayed centuries of scurrying and frenetic activity. In small details – a brass lantern, a knife sharpening block, a faded inscription – Corran could sense the presence of many generations of Mori: father, grandfather, great-grandfather.

Contemporary establishments in fashionable downtown Tokyo had affected to emulate such a look, recreating the appearance of 'antiquity' in modern materials and fabrics. But these were mere surface cosmetics, any attempt at real character or ambience betrayed by cheap textures and synthetic effects.

Knowing that he only had minutes inside, Corran shook such aesthetic concerns from his thoughts and scanned the room. Baskets of river ginger, goma seeds and dried shiitake mushrooms hung from a wooden trestle that occupied most of the far wall. Neatly arranged over the work surface were sacks of Kochi rice, wakeme seaweed, napa cabbage and lime-green Sansho peppers. To the right, above thick chopping blocks, several shelves were stacked with hand-hammered woks, old pots and glass jars. Ceramic vessels contained gingko nuts, niva chives and lotus root.

Corran, impressed by the variety of ingredients, examined the numerous containers and bowls. Yes they were rare, some had even come from remote locations (he noticed red Azuki beans from Yunnan), but they were mostly known to him – nothing was that unusual or surprising.

In the far corner of the modest space, a worn, ornate Shinto cabinet caught his eye. He opened the main doors. Inside, carved picture frames depicted images of the Takeshi clan, their homes, families and meagre possessions. The faded sepia prints revealed another era; a past before mechanisation, of street scenes, geisha girls standing against elegant painted backdrops of cherry blossom, local sumo wrestlers and fishing boats lining the wharf almost a century earlier than the commercial port that now dominated the area.

Nestling amongst the photo frames was a small shrine. Incense sticks smouldered in bronze burners, shaped in the form of mythical dragons. An aura of reverence surrounded the cabinet. That was nice, reflected Corran; Mori was either a fool or a comic to draw attention to it. Heritage, tradition, the ways of the ancestors – it was so obvious it was almost a cliche. A bright neon sign might have drawn less attention.

There were four small doors on the front of the cabinet. The most prominent, the one more obviously worn and used, was locked. Bizarrely the key was still in place. He turned the lock and opened the door. On a narrow shelf inside rested a single vessel; a tin container with a printed symbol of a bicycle on the front as if it were machine oil. Obviously more of Mori's puerile trickery thought Corran. Reaching for the glass bottle, he unscrewed the top, dipped a finger in the sauce and tasted. His body twisted up in disgust; the flavour unearthly, utterly repugnant, scorched his tongue.

Spitting the residue onto the floor he searched for water to wash the inside of his mouth. His eyes fell by chance to the side of Mori's raised workstation. He saw a second container; a red plastic bottle, as plain and ordinary as the other was exotic. One sniff was enough to confirm it was what he was looking for. Corran laughed softly to himself: in his panic, his rush to be out, the dumb fool had stupidly left his crucial secret in plain sight, in the open.

Concealing the precious bottle in the folds of his linen jacket, Corran's thoughts turned to escape. Once through the separating curtain, it looked good. He could hear the kitchen staff outside, still distracted by whatever commotion Jade had so dramatically orchestrated. He must only have been seconds inside. The corridor was empty. He'd made a clean getaway. He could relax.

Waiting for the voices on the veranda to subside, Corran was about to turn again for the main restaurant when a soft, almost imperceptible hum caught his attention. He turned around. A small distant doorway at the far end of the corridor was partly open. Peering through the gap in the door, he saw an angelic face, the face of a child. Their eyes met. He smiled and shrugged his shoulders; the innocuous look of a dumb foreigner who had stupidly got lost on the way back from the restroom. For seconds it looked as if his play acting had worked and he had secured her silence; he thought she smiled back. But then, for no clear reason, this sweet, cherubic little thing, shrieked like the Devil's only child; a high pitched, blood curdling scream, loud enough to wake the Takeshi dead.

Rudely jolted from his state of surety, Corran knew he was in serious trouble. He turned and rushed back down the corridor towards the dining area. Against all earthly logic, the howl from the back of the store room appeared to lift in intensity the further he got from the kitchen. How such a small girl could have so much volume in her lungs was remarkable.

Corran chose a second route back to the veranda. Although it brought him out on the far side of the kitchen block and away from the petulant child, the frustratingly short distance back to his table was blocked by an overturned table and chair. Plates, glasses and food littered the floorboards. Obviously Jade's work; impressive, though maybe a touch excessive. Strangely she was nowhere to be seen. Instead Mori's people were everywhere. Three were on their knees, clearing up the broken plates and glasses. Two more were sweeping food from the floor, another picked up fragments from a broken vase.

Corran, anxious to remain in the shadows, edged away from the upturned furniture. He failed to notice a streak of dark, sticky sauce that had seeped across the boards. Slipping on the vicious fluid he glided softly, like an inelegant ice skater into the doors of a glass cabinet. The slight tinkle of glass would have gone unnoticed, had not the sound occurred at the exact same moment that the shrieking child ran out of steam. Every eye in the place turned in the direction of the faint vibration. In the gloom of the corridor, they saw Corran, looking sheepish, arms wrapped around the fragile cabinet in a frenzied attempt to smother the ringing glass.

Mori's men moved quickly to block the exits over the bridge and the corridor to the back. Several diners, already sensing trouble had risen from their seats and were retreating into the shadows. A nervous banker, abandoning all pretence of being a local, was already on his mobile anxiously calling for his chauffeur.

Mori himself stood to Corran's right. As his long silver hair lifted in the breeze, the old man pointed to his side and barked an order. The kitchen staff closed in a ring around Corran. The two stockiest to the left were the immediate concern. One was swinging a meat cleaver. Spurred on by Mori, this short fat man shuffled nearer to Corran. Ironically it was a third person, older and lankier than the 'sumo sized' half-back, who appeared the most menacing. What caught

Corran's eye were the Russian Special forces tattoos that ran down the length of his fore arms; he must have done time in a Soviet naval base kitchen – probably Vladivostok. Perversely Corran went straight for him, figuring that by age and weight he would have the advantage. He was wrong. As Corran raced forward, the old man grabbed his arm, effortlessly lifted him from the ground and swung him violently across the floor. Corran landed with a painful crunch against the boards.

Recovering, Corran quickly sized up the situation. His options were rapidly dwindling. He could make a break for it over the small bridge to the pier (the two waiters stationed there didn't look much of a threat), or he could go over the side into the sea. Seconds later the first option was already off the escape list. Staff from a neighbouring restaurant had come in support, some wielding warlike rolling pins. Six of them now blocked the bridge to the market. Clearly he couldn't make it through. His only option was the water. But for seconds he dithered; his nervous vacillation, sizing up the jump, fearing to commit, making him perform an unusual bobbing action. The soles of his squeaky trainers, straining first to the left and then to the right, sounded like a panicked cartoon duck, drawing nervous laughs from the remaining diners. But Mori wasn't fooled. Immediately anticipating Corran's dilemma, he screamed out another directive. Two of his men ran towards the railing. Corran, seeing his only remaining avenue of escape being closed off, moved faster. Leaping to his feet he dodged a blow from the reedy Russian Special Forces chef, slipped nimbly between the two fat sumo men and threw himself over the side.

It was further than he thought. Since arriving the tide must have gone out. He landed badly, hitting rocks only metres below the surface. Abruptly entering the water two things came to mind with lucid, cinematic clarity. Firstly it was fiercely, bitterly cold. Secondly, a knife – an expensive and rare Ryusen blade – a cherished possession of any reputable chef), sliced through the water inches from his face. In focusing on the elegant blade, Corran, twisting over in the water, allowed the bottle to slip from his jacket pocket. Turning too late, he saw the precious sauce disappear into the murky depths.

Two

Corran emerged from the sea on a rough pebble beach sandwiched between two fishing wharfs. Sliding on mountains of waste – ropes, trainers and bottles mixed in a greasy stew of seaweed, engine effluents and putrefying fish waste – he scrambled up the slippery incline.

He'd taken his time in the waves. Of course he was scared. The thought of fighting it out with a small army of knife-wielding butchers was enough to keep him submerged between the columns of the pier despite the numbing cold. Mori in his anger had been relentless. Pounding up and down the walkways, he had leant over the railings and scanned the inky depths with a powerful LED torch. Only the sight of his timorous diners, anxiously waiting to complete their meals, had coerced him to give up. Although the violence had undoubtedly shaken some (the fury with which Mori had thrown his precious blade had been particularly unsettling), few were prepared to sacrifice their chance to sample Mori's signature dish – snowflakes of frozen sake, sprinkled over slices of green strawberry and juniper berries, accented with an arc of cayenne pepper; all staged on a strip of cedar wood – reputed to be the seminal highlight of the meal.

Corran, reaching the top of the beach, took some time to reflect on his condition; the worst case scenario – he often did that when he was in a fix – a need to reframe his sense of self within his universe of one. He looked a mess. And, covered in oily, rancid seaweed, he stank. The hotel was miles away. Being so shaken and rattled, he even had trouble remembering its name – Chu, Shimi, Shimbu something. Of course, he had the contact number in his mobile, but he'd lost that in the fall. That was no big deal. It wasn't a smartphone. It was a cheap disposable Samsung he had picked up at the airport to make local calls. It was probably resting at the bottom of the harbour. Irretrievable. As was the bottle. That hurt the most. He'd been desperate to uncover Mori's secret. But this time, he'd had to admit, he'd totally overplayed his hand. What was he thinking? The fight must have been some kind of strange aberration. He'd never fought anyone in his life. How he thought he could possibly have taken on any of them, let alone win, was a mystery; a dangerous delusion he had probably picked up from playing too many mindless computer games on long haul flights. And the knife, the Ryusen blade Mori had thrown at him in the water; with a reputation for slicing the fineness slithers of sushi, it would have gone straight through him.

On the plus side, there were small comforts. He'd been able to decipher at least two of Mori's recipes: the scallop *wasabia* and the Wagyu *gyoza*. And the chief thing was he hadn't been recognised. They didn't know who he was. The reservation was in Jade's name.

Where was Jade? A quick glance at the low wall fronting the promenade, where they had parked the Audi, now empty, showed that she had long gone. Corran winced with the memory of how he had used her. After all the time and effort she had put in to arranging the evening, his behaviour had been at best, appalling.

There was talk she was out to seduce him. This was less credible. Corran was aware she had a boyfriend. He was an entrepreneur who invested in nightclubs and Korean boybands. Yes, he was short, but he wasn't bad looking, bought her expensive jewellery and had mentioned a penthouse apartment they were buying together. Nevertheless, Corran had to admit, on the few times he had met Jade, she had been especially attentive. And the designer dress, betrayed by its pristine folds, looked like it was straight off the shelves; obviously purchased to impress. Maybe he had led her on. Friends had accused him of flirting with Jade only because of her influence with people in high places. In reality, his motives were blunter, purely mercenary: to get into the notorious Hiro San. And Jade's uncle knew Mori. It was Corran's only chance to get a table. A rare opportunity to explore Mori's recipes. Of course, in that he had miserably failed. Whatever was bound up in that special bottle was now gone, lost in the sea. Time to give up. It was over. In twenty-four hours he'd be in Bangkok.

Grey clouds scudding across the horizon, broke momentarily. The moon cut through. Just to the east of the glowing disc he noticed an intense light in the sky. For seconds it looked like a satellite. But it clearly didn't move; it was probably a planet.

Corran wrung the last water from his jacket. Scrambling up the steep bank and falling in the seaweed, something caught his eye in the waves. It was the distinctive red bottle, bouncing at the edge of the surf.

Three

Font Lescari, one of New York's oldest publishing houses, was founded in the late 19th century by two unlikely entrepreneurs: a retired Scottish whaling captain and an Italian station clerk. Starting from an unpromising title list made up mostly of freight timetables and shipping manifests (which in its own small way narrated a history of time, people and stuff), the firm went on to build an empire from piggy backing off the communications advance of the time-telephony and the incorporated need for number directories. Comfortable with their content niche, the presses rolled day and night and the revenues flowed. It was only after one of their Sales Directors got marooned on a train for a day with nothing but the Chicago 4th district as reading matter, that they resolved to print something more enlightening. They opened a small publishing arm and took risks with the first wave of post-war writing talent soon to form the vanguard of the Beat Generation; writers such as Ron Mead, Sarah Mitchell and the *Time Life* war correspondent, Bruce Miller. Although its authors had come under fire for their 'liberal affiliations', a mistrust fuelled by the suspicions of the Cold War, Font Lescari had refused to be strong-armed by the scare-mongering of the extreme right and the ensuing climate of fear. With media companies and film studios wilfully surrendering their writers and talent to the witch-hunt, the Lescari editors had been persistent in their support of authors deemed 'damaging to American values' (their maintenance team had even built a 'priest hole' in their Newark distribution warehouse, stocked up with enough corned beef and Budweiser beer to last out for more than a month). When these political fears receded in the mid-seventies, the publishing house, recognised for its ideological stand, grew wealthy on the authors who stayed loyal despite the lure of higher advances from larger, more aggressive rivals. But that was the past.

The dawn of the twenty first-century had been a rude awakening for the Lescari Group. Blind to the threat of the technological age, with its 'weapons of smart distribution' – mobile phones, tablets and ebooks – the silver-haired company Directors, slow to stem the erosion of their revenues, had found themselves at the mercy of a far younger tech-savvy generation. Loudly proclaiming the death of the old paper publishing model, a rush of media consultants and business strategists surged through the revolving doors of the formerly salubrious, Broadway offices. Radical new 'disruptive' prescriptions were promised to re-educate and reboot the aged Lescari management team into the ways of the digital age. Dismissive of past knowledge and experience, the fresh-faced iconoclasts – peddling new revenue models and data-visualisations that wouldn't look out of place in an episode of Star Trek – charted a radical new roadmap to the future.

Obedient to theories of 'hockey-stick growth', the trend was on for larger, more aggressive titles; titles that could be amplified and inflated by the collective hot air of a million tweets and social media 'likes'. With no interest in fighting it out for shelf space, Big Data became the black arts of strategy. Rapid, viral scale was the measure of success; the No 1 best seller-all or nothing.

Putting an axe to the 'mid list', projects considered too lame or weak to generate the necessary incendiary buzz, Lescari's bright young minds had banked the future of the company on the success of, essentially, three titles. The first was from an former Lehman Brothers executive, Sheila Bernharht. Bernharht's revelations, first aired in a New Year edition of *Forbes* magazine, had shaken many with her disquieting and lurid revelations of some of the world's foremost banks at the heart of the global financial crisis. Crazed by a belief that they were truly starring into the mouth of the abyss, coked-up executives had indulged in an orgy of guns, girls and gangsters, that had culminated in a surreal plan to conceal their cataclysmic losses by taking out the Wall Street stock exchange. A chauffeur, who worked for the board of Directors, was intercepted off Interstate 87 with half a ton of fertiliser wrapped in the boot of his stretched Mercedes. The plan, comic-book crude, was to blame the atrocity on middle-eastern jihadists.

The second project was Lee Fajun's controversial exposé of China's economic miracle and the illusion of the country's growth. Fajun's account was deemed so damaging to the upper party echelon and its legions of billionaire tycoons across the globe, that it was rumoured that Beijing had dispatched a hit squad to silence the offensive author. Having survived what appeared to be a messy assassination attempt at a Chinese noodle bar in Greenwich Village (few had considered that this might have been a publicity stunt dreamt up by his wife's promotion company; a video had played live on Snapchat), Fajun's book had been instantly propelled to the top of the best-seller list across three continents.

Corran Brook's book was the third project in Lescari's ambitious new line-up.

Corran had come to the world of *haute cuisine* by mistake. His father, a criminal barrister, had wanted his son to enter the legal profession – it ran in the family. But in his finals Corran had achieved the dubious honour of scraping through with the lowest possible mark ever recorded for a degree in the history of the national university. His parents, shocked by his dismal failure, had interviewed his faculty tutor to insist on Corran being reassessed. Might there have been some kind of mix-up?

When his papers had been retrieved, the true depths of Corran's failure were self evident; most had had to concur that his assessors had been surprisingly lenient. Later it was discovered that behind this fall was a girl. Of course there was nothing unusual about pupils failing academically because of a university infatuation. What had really messed up his psyche, and specifically his inability to master his economics stats, was the shock that she had been sleeping with eight other graduates, all considered among the brightest of the year. More damaging still, three were close friends. Gossip speculated that for the girl to weave together such a complex schedule of lies, meetings, dinners and bedroom liaisons with so many for so long without being discovered, must have involved some pretty astute proprietary software, worthy of a doctorate in its own right.

The girl was Lucy Mecker, an Italian-American, politics and economics student. Mecker had taken to extremes the advice that if you wanted to be truly smart you needed to mix with smart people. Sleeping with them, she considered, was as close as you could get. But what had innocently started as a late night dare between her more adventurous room mates, developed into a darker power play. She fought with the dangerous notion that there might be some truth to it; that by passionate love-making she could sap the intellectual vigour from her victims. Rationally the idea was absurd and she knew it. Yet her grades always reflected a clear boost after such trysts. And her success in her finals, a double first with honours, only added toxicity to a corrupting notion, that would, later in life, evolve into an all consuming, vampirish and damaging mania.

The fall out for Corran's eight associates was more extensive. All had failed. Despite official complaints to the board of governors, the predatory Mecker had sailed through the controversy without a blemish to her record. Corran later learnt that she had entered the foreign office; fast tracked to a first posting in Moscow where she had become deputy and within months, the Cultural Attaché. Whenever international newspapers headlined a story about a diplomat's spectacular fall from grace, Corran, sensitive to his own emotional wounds, imagined Mecker's signature behind it.

Yet Corran, in his own way, wasn't totally scarred by this early trauma. When people talked about drive and ambition, Corran could not deny that Mecker had provided some, if not all, of the initial powder.

Despite his low grades, Corran scrapped a place at Colombia in New York to study sociology. But his heart wasn't in it. After a disillusioning first year he dropped out. Following in the footsteps of his fictional hero, Sal Paradise in Kerouac's '*On The Road*', he headed west, picking up manual work drifting across Colorado and Arizona. At his lowest ebb he took a job dressed as a 'Blackberry Fruit Fool', promoting frozen yogurt for a local supermarket chain on Venice Beach. A passing restaurant manager, far from recognising his talents (other than being able to sustain roasting temperatures in a vulcanised rubber suit – a skill set possibly only of use to Nasa astronauts and iron foundry workers), felt distraught that anyone had to accept so much humiliation for so little reward. Purely to relieve him of his ordeal, he offered him a job as a dishwasher in his Italian restaurant. Bidding goodbye to his sticky purple jump suit with a viking burial off the Santa Monica Pier, Corran gratefully accepted the position.

The restaurant was in the hills above West Hollywood. It looked serene and relaxed; the location high enough to catch a cooling afternoon breeze. Ironically the heat was even more intense, the hours longer, the conditions airless and insanitary, making his degradation yet more complete. He was treated like pond life, the lowest of the low. Orders and instructions were shouted at him through a small hatch in the wall, as if he were a badly trained dog. Yet Corran thrived. Looking from the black hole of his scullery to the kitchen, where there were gleaming polished work stations, rows of ordered copper pans, walk-in fridges and stainless steel sous-vide ovens, he caught a glimpse of where and what he wanted to be.

Canali was no ordinary dining venue. Opened for two years and still a well kept secret within the affluent art gallery clique, it was already courting its first Michelin star. Corran, with a reputation for maintaining a cheery disposition despite the demeaning tasks thrown at him, quietly bided his time. When a position as under-chief became available, he applied and was appointed. Soaking up all the practical and theoretical knowledge he could find, he amazed the other kitchen staff with his relentless thirst for learning. The first to arrive for work and the last to leave, he filled every spare minute between his official tasks experimenting over a hot stove.

With Canali's reputation spreading across the state, a local cable channel, producing a mini-series on the most promising new restaurant start-ups, arranged to film an interview with the key staff. Through a mix-up in the scheduling, the cable crew managed to turn up on the one day that the restaurant was closed. Corran, having worked through the night on his own designs, was asleep on packaging in the storeroom when he heard the hammering on the front door. He was the only one on the premises to let them in. Panicked calls were made. Nino Nostromo, Canali's head chef, three hundred miles away at a wine festival in Soneva Valley, refused to cut short his visit to make the trip south. The producer, already under pressure to head to his second location, the best steamed Bao buns on the beach, desperately searched for a solution. He didn't have to look far; Corran, stretching the truth as to his true position and experience, brazenly, and wrongly (in retrospect), offered to step in. The programme was aired a month later. Though Corran couldn't have been held responsible for the edit, it was self-evident from the opening shot he would be fired.

Taking part time work in a sandwich bar, Corran was forced to temporarily shelve his culinary ambitions. But he was not entirely forgotten. When the cable producer moved to an Internet network, he remembered the cocky young 'pretender' and called Corran up. His first show, 'Great in Sixty Seconds', was a cooking programme designed to persuade kids that they could make healthy food in the same time it took to order a McDonald's. Though it barely registered in the ratings, Corran had found himself on the inside of the big sound-proofed studio door with the red flashing light 'on air' and he wasn't turning back. He looked good on camera, could run through a half-hour programme almost unscripted and pasted over his lack of experience with raw energy and enthusiasm.

He was never a great chef. And in an age when every culinary star claimed to be exploring some creative new frontier, he'd be the first to admit that he never had an original idea in his head – he had no wealth within. Deep thinking and abstract mental juggling he found a burden. He didn't have the patience or the time for it. But in the connected world, the thought processor of the collective mind, was invention entirely necessary? Inspiration was everywhere; more than a million recipes for a boiled egg. Remixed, reordered, reimagined, he could give the semblance of originality without the heavy lifting.

Two series later, two books published and a line of cooking utensils to his name, Corran returned to Sydney with aspirations beyond the confines of the salaried studio chef.

Looking to recast himself in a greater guise, Corran reinvented himself as a 'gastronaut'. Taking a lead from anthropologists who scoured forgotten corners to preserve dying languages, beliefs and cultures, Corran planned to do the same for cuisine. From Archangel to Zanibar, he searched out remote destinations, towns and villages, to unearth forgotten recipes and traditional cooking methods at threat from being smothered by the relentless march of progress and its accompanying legions of supermarket chains and fast-food franchises.

Recording ideas handed down over generations, Corran became like a forensic detective, unearthing strange, often magical secrets and revelations from people who had remained doggedly loyalty to the ways of their forebears. His charm was to win the confidence of the wizened wives and grandmothers, joking and cackling behind steaming cauldrons, who in harbouring such knowledge, recognised that they might have to put aside their age-old distrust of foreigners in order to pass on their dying skills (their children having long abandoned the villages for the bright lights of the city).

It was food with a timeless quality, embodying the virtues of the land in which they lived; the nutrients within the soil, the water, the trees (and sometimes spirits) that made up their home and their surroundings. Small nuances were important; the suggestion that a wooden pestle (in one case a rare Leopard wood), or even the shape and age of a bowl, might have an impact, on the final taste of a dish.

For Western minds disenchanted with a world of plenty, such narratives came as a welcome antidote to the ubiquity and waste of tasteless consumerism. As a corrective to the faceless rapaciousness of the giant multinationals, Corran cast a light on forgotten folk beliefs, where there was still integrity, truth and respect for the land.

Of course, the idea of chef as anthropologist wasn't new. Many of his 'wild, off-the-map' locations had already done mainstream TV – one even had an Apple store. But Corran refreshed the genre by positioning himself as an intrepid, often reckless, adventurer; a Bear Grylls with a frying pan.

Covering a segment in Kashmir, Corran had hunted down a former terrorist who ran a cafe from the back of his Tacoma pick-up truck (known as a 'technical' in the trade – its 12 mm machine-gun having been replaced with a kebab grill). Night-time lenses and hidden cameras had made much of him sneaking across the India-Pakistan border despite there being a conventional check-point.

To highlight his grit, ancient ceremonies were often dusted off, reinvented or totally invented, so that Corran could share in some drug crazed ritual to secure the trust of a tribe and obtain some lucrative footage. In one unsettling incident, shamans had led Corran's crew into a warren of caves to an 'underworld', where they had attempted to summon up the spirit of a long-dead ancestor to reveal a forgotten recipe for wood bison. Perhaps it was the drop in temperature, but a cold chill went down Corran's spine. Somehow a vision did occur. Flames leapt up from the darkest recesses of the cave. A crude vessel hovered above the fire. Corran caught the powerful aroma of flesh and cinnamon. Actually it smelt burnt. Would the undead have overcooked such an mythical recipe?

His shows were successful. A feature on the Siberian Naukan, living off fermented walrus intestine, made the news on CNN. A Tibetan woman he recorded in the Ronghu Valley, produced a meal whose dishes unfolded like a narrative. Each course represented a cast of characters, woven together into a complex myth of her people and ancestors, living in the romantic peach groves of the Shang mountains.

Living with the Philippine Balut, he had discovered an old man who communed with birds and bees to guide him on his foraging expeditions. His method, deemed crazy at the time, was later borne out by botanists; certain plants attracted particular bird and insect activity. The programme went on to inspire a free-food movement in Portland, Oregon. The community used bird-song recordings to communicate certain 'phrases' with their feathered friends, who in turn, helped them in their hunt for wild berries and fruit.

Four years later, Corran had amassed an extraordinary archive of more than three-thousand hours of recordings and videos. He returned to his Sydney harbour kitchen, together with hundreds of previously unrecorded ingredients, herbs. spices and plants. It was these unique discoveries and methods that, once perfected and adapted to modern cooking processes, lifted him further into the media limelight. His mix of lost horizons, culinary forensics, and chef as cultural protector and guardian, paid dividends.

But with success came criticism. Social commentators and academics, envious and out to discredit, questioned his motives and altruism. Far from preserving old traditions, Corran was accused of looting the heritage of others, packaging and canning it like so many peach slices, for his own material gain. 'Cultural appropriation' was the damning term used. A class-action lawsuit, taken out by a human-rights lawyer in Hawaii, fighting for the rights of a South Sea Island community (already in danger from sea level rise), threatened to put a dent in his enterprise. Corran countered by arguing that he was doing no more than other recorders of antiquity; archeologists who preserved rare artefacts in museums, photographers who captured images of primitive tribes and rock stars who saved moribund careers by recordings albums with desert nomads.

Such controversies only lifted Corran's star to greater prominence. Soon after, the deal with Font Lescari was secured. Both the CEO, Henry Gaze, and the commissioning editor, Teddy Callister, flew out to Sydney to discuss the concept and strategy for his forthcoming title, *The Story of Food*. After two days sleeping by the pool to recover from jetlag, the Font Lescari executives invited Corran to a presentation at a private conference room in their hotel, where they talked up the project with the fervour of rocket scientists gunning for Mars. They weren't into 'books', they were into 'properties'. The vision for the publication would be truly global. This was a title that, rather than focusing on a particular cuisine, would celebrate a shared world heritage. The concept of countries and borders was discarded. Food types, their movement and migration around the globe, would be the framework that better reflected the rich diversity of ideas and methods. And it would be comprehensive. The dominant culinary empires of the western world would share space with the lost and forgotten.

Callister's team had done a good job. Having methodically played through every frame of Corran's documentary series, they had drawn up a value list that perfectly aligned with his own sensibilities. And just in case Corran might harbour any lingering doubts that they weren't the right guys to go with (they were aware that Random House and Bertelsmann had also made informal advances), they assured Corran that behind the scenes, his teams would ensure that 'The Story of Food', (from Adam and Eve to El Bulli), wouldn't just arrive as yet another decorative celebrity title. It would be the publishing sensation of the year.

Corran was impressed. Though at first a touch daunted by the evangelical intensity of the Font Lescari team (two of the sales directors had concluded their pitch with a Kanye West inspired rap act), a casual aside as to the size of his advance at a drinks party after the presentation was enough to secure his signature on the contract.

Riding in on their zeal, Corran cleared his schedule and devoted two months to the first two chapters of the book. Designers and photographers were brought in. These early spreads, together with a format for the book, were presented to the publishers in their New York offices.

Though described as a 'work in progress', the designs more than satisfied. Gaze was so taken by the radical nature of the book that he arranged for a mock-up to be shown to the main share holders at an investor meeting. Carl Lindberg, fresh from his sale of the Met Music Group, invited Corran to cook for a handful of his acquaintances and neighbours at his Shelter Island retreat. Cooking from a portable kitchen built over the pebble beach, Corran grilled buffalo steaks, served on a bed of edamame crisps and edible bank notes. Later, relaxed on a deck chair, he looked on as Washington senators and lingerie models smoked joints and danced naked until dawn.

San Francisco was scoped out to explore the latest digital advances. Lunch and learn sessions with Silicon Valley tech gurus were capped by long, languid dinners in hill-top hideaways. Seduced by the love and attention, more introductions followed. Corran enjoyed his new Californian friends; everyone shooting so high – the next George Clooney, Rihanna, Kendal Jenner. And when such impossible dreams faltered, they drifted downstream, latching onto the successes of others, becoming trainers, happiness gurus, pool attendants and dog walkers to the stars.

Passed between addresses in Malibu and Sunset Boulevard, each more hedonistic than the first, he was beginning to believe that the hard work was already done.

Returning to Sydney was a shock. It was mid winter. Hail had fallen on the harbour-front. His restaurants looked tired and neglected. Hating the harsh weather, Corran returned to his Bay Park offices with a gnawing unease. Seduced by the drive and passion of the New Yorkers, a Disney-like alter reality had taken hold. A thousand, promised 'yes we cans' morphed into a collective 'no we can't'. He had over-reached himself.

Worse still, when he opened his laptop and was presented by a fresh screen, nothing came. All the months of positivity, ideation and brain-storming, now kindled nothing but emptiness and despair.

His archive, a wall of shining stainless-steel filling cabinets, looked impressive, but inside was a mess. Gaping holes in his research were discovered. Although the more obscure and distant outposts of the world were more than aptly represented (including one hundred inventive recipes for Inuit seal meat), there were some embarrassing and fundamental omissions. In his anxiety to be original, the most visited cities in Southeast Asia – Shanghai, Tokyo and Bangkok – perversely within his known sphere of operation, weren't even covered.

After several sleepless nights, Corran skyped New York in a vain attempt to buy some time. Font Lescari didn't like the timbre of his call. With TV shows, magazine spreads and supermarket deals etched in stone, shifting the schedule was like slowing a runaway train. Adamant that the deadlines couldn't be altered, their answer was to throw money and people at it – more assistants, photographers and writers. To still Corran's concerns, it was decided that the simplest solution was to combine the cities which he still had to research, with a series of pre-publicity tours. Although it bought Corran more time, it did little to alleviate his building tension and anxiety.

The debacle at Hiro San had been painful enough. But the half-hour submerged in the miserable chill waters of Chiba harbour had left him with a persistent fever that no amount of modern medicine could shake off. He was also experiencing late-night anxiety fits, the intensity of which he hadn't encountered since his dark days at Columbia. By the time he had left Tokyo for Bangkok, he had slipped even further behind with his manuscript. After a long flight delay from Narita, he gained a modicum of relief by being met at Suvarnabhumi airport by his PR agent from Sydney, Amy Miller.

Amy had been brought in by Corran to organise the Southeast Asian tour. It was a Lescari idea to bring her in early to provide some much needed sanity and calm.

Taken by Amy to a river-side hotel in the heart of the city, he slept for twenty-four hours.

Four

Corran had met Amy Carlyle in Dharamsala. Just two months clear of her finals and having worked a long, dry summer on the festival circuit, she had saved enough money to fulfil her dream of doing a round the world tour with her boyfriend. More than seeing different countries and cultures she wanted to expose herself to deeper, more challenging experiences before settling for a sober, perhaps for ever, conventional career glued to a computer screen, Pret A Manger sandwiches the default lunch.

In her cramp bedsit in Kennington, south London, Amy had meticulously pinned a circle of coloured flags on a map of the world. Starting in Europe, then winding through Asia followed by Australia, the route jumped to the west coast of South America, finishing in the Galapagos islands (a childhood ambition to swim with Darwin's Marine Iguanas).

Somehow it hadn't worked out. After torrential rains had seen them holed up in a youth hostel in a mud-clogged hill station in Sikkim (only the third pin on the board), the boyfriend, demoralised by the heat, the unfamiliar food and the lack of connectivity, was loath to continue. With stomach cramps, an alarming purple allergy rash that ran down the right side of his chest, his face riddled with mosquito bites, he surrendered to the oppressive climate, bed-bugs and malevolent gods and secretly packed his backpack. The following day he walked out on Amy (annoyingly unscathed by his catalogue of afflictions) and went home.

Amy, feeling like a dead weight had been cut from her shoulders, stayed and worked for a local tour group organising treks to the Kangra valley and the outer Himalayas. Corran, overnighting in Dharmsala after a flight had been postponed because of fog, persuaded her to work for him. It began with simple admin – logging DHL mail, booking hotels, arranging transport and organising visas.

When Corran returned to his Sydney office, she followed. Her first week in his harbour-front offices (in fact her first week in any office) was unsettling. Presented with a work-station, a desktop PC, filing cabinets and preprinted business cards, she panicked. Commitment, responsibility, a thirty seven hour working week, wasn't this everything she had run away from when she set off from grimy Kennington? Hadn't she told friends and family that she wanted to see the world, experience mind-bending drugs, discover her inner nature?

Struggling with the seat adjustments on her new executive chair, she realised how little she knew; virtually nothing about management, even less about cooking, zero on publishing. The existing staff were civil enough, helping out where they could – but she sensed hidden resentment over her close relationship with their boss. Lively conversations around the coffee point muted when she walked by.

But as the weeks passed and her discomforts eased (mastering her Herman Miller chair was a turning point), rather than feeling intimidated by this alien new world of staff meetings, budget projections, weekly reviews and reports, she felt strangely empowered. Yes she could play the global drifter – her bright blue eyes, brown freckles and lightly flowing auburn hair had always given her an air of dizzy detachment – but it was a surface superficiality that, unrealised even by herself, masked a latent middle manager inside: precise, well ordered, a-z indexed. At first such an admission made her feel guilty; ashamed that she felt more affinity for word docs and spreadsheets than ashrams and yoga retreats. But did every spiritual quest have to end with Nirvana?

If she had enquired further she would have found answers in her genealogy. Her Scottish grandfather was a daunting Methodist minister, who lived out his life battling idolatry on a remote Polynesian island by torching their devilish sculptures and carvings (although later in life more profitably sold to the British Museum). Amy never knew him. But his portrait – thin sallow face framed by a grey, turbulent beard (dense enough to provide nesting for colonies of small tropical birds) – dominated the hall of their austere childhood home. Passing by this image on the way to school with her younger brothers, his mean, beady eyes seemed to bore into their souls, searching out every minor transgression. With such a puritanical work ethic burnt into her psyche, Amy never missed a day of school, lost her homework or dropped an exam. Pointed in the right direction she was dogged and indefatigable.

When the head of PR left to have a baby, Corran encouraged Amy to take the job. Eagerly accepting, she threw herself into the role, crowning her first week with a series of embarrassing and obvious mistakes: she sent a Japanese interpreter to greet a delegation of Korean bankers, while expensive Dublin Bay langoustine, sent in all the way from Otter Bay, Fraserburgh, West Scotland, were sent back to Otter Bay, Fraserburgh, West Scotland.

Going against prevailing gossip that she would be out before the end of the month, Corran ironically warmed to her particular blend of diligence and chaos. New to the business, Amy had a raw enthusiasm, an uncorrupted, unquestioning 'yes can do' positivity that meant that she never baulked at even his most outrageous and, often, frivolous demands. Her's was an innocence that looked at problems with fresh eyes; enjoying challenges that would have ground down and exhausted her more experienced and jaded office colleagues.

Thinking she would only last two weeks, she more than survived, she thrived. Two years went by. When Font Lescari green lighted the Southeast Asian tour, Corran called Amy into the office.

"I want you to organise the tour."

He had said it quickly, with no preamble before she had even had time to take a seat. Covering her face, she looked close to crying. Initially, Corran was worried that he had pushed her too far, too fast and she was having some sort of meltdown. But it was more complicated than that. It was an emotional reaction against years of naysayers; from boyfriends to course tutors, even the critical glare of her Grandfather's ghost, telling her she was no good. The catty office rumours only confirmed these anxieties. Conditioned to expecting the worse, she thought her failings had finally caught up with her, that her time was up, the guillotine set. Called into the office, the tears were already there, primed, ready to flow. Good or bad news there was going to be a dramatic outburst.

Wiping away the tears streaming down her face, she hugged Corran. Of course, she would accept. The destinations were all on her wish list. It would give her the chance to finally finish the trip she had promised herself as a backpacker (she planned to send her old, lacklustre boyfriend a 'wish you weren't here' postcard from each destination).

The publicity tour started in Bangkok. More than Hong Kong, Singapore even Beijing, Corran had chosen the city, not purely because it lay geographically at the centre of the Asian food universe, but because, in all honesty, he just loved Thai food more. From backstreet stall to suburban kitchen or palace cuisine (he had once eaten in a grand, but termite-infested villa of a minor Thai prince), good food was everywhere. The Roof Terrace restaurant, perched on the fifty-fifth floor of the newly-built, Carlton Wattana Tower, in Bangkok's affluent residential district, was selected as the venue.

At the river-side hotel, a spare bedroom adjacent to Corran's suite was found as a temporary office. Even before Amy had entered the room, she had played through in her mind just how she wanted to arrange it. A white board and a filing cabinet had been found by the reception staff in the basement. She had bought batches of coloured post-it notes and marker pens from Sydney. The map from her aborted student trip had been rescued from her back pack. Marking the new destinations, Nong Khai, Luang Prabang, Siem Riep, and Hanoi with the same distinctive red pins she had kept from London, her sense of adventure and excitement returned.

Getting access to Corran's correspondence was her idea. She thought it wise to add her name to the shared emails from the New York production team. Seconds later it didn't seem so smart. Pointlessly complicated with comments, attachments and links, it took her most of the morning to sort through the 'need to know' essentials from the mountains of bureaucratic fluff. And from these remaining messages, a deepening picture of disorder began to emerge – text and documents had gone missing, image requests from the digital team had been ignored, urgent deadlines gone unheeded.

Senior Lescari executives such Gaze and Callister had attempted to intervene. Even these 'friendly' nudges had gone unread. Where Corran had made rare responses, his monosyllabic replies – "no!", "why?", "what the *!", only raised the temperature of the exchanges. Amy could sense enough friction to spark a small fire. Maybe such an inferno was, at that moment, winging its way across the Atlantic.

Needing a break from the screen, Amy shut down her laptop, grabbed a towel and bikini and headed for the garden. The long emerald-green pool, shaded by lush palms and ferns, was colder than she expected. No wonder she was the only swimmer. By the time she had made the turn into her sixtieth lap, the reason why she had been flown out to Bangkok a week earlier than planned became clear. Corran's pet project was unravelling. She was firefighting. It made her reflect on the ease with which she had been offered the role in the first place. There had been three other candidates at the time. All were more senior and experienced. Two had sudden work commitments. The other claimed to have booked major dental surgery at the last minute. Had she only really been chosen because others, wise to the crisis, had run scared?

Brooding on these suspicions, anger that she might have been manipulated, somehow outwitted, only hardened her resolve. Although she had only just towelled herself dry, she sprinted up the service stairs to the tenth floor, getting sticky and hot again with the exertion.

Back in her room, a double espresso provided the hard reset. Methodically she began answering the most pressing concerns from New York. The majority focused on the all-important launch party. There was less than a week to organise the event. Of course, invitations to the media and the essential journalists had been sent out, but it all needed to be confirmed. The most embarrassing oversight was that although the event was billed as a major book launch, there were no books. Corran hadn't finished and the Lescari management had decided to bluff it. Working through the night, the production team had painstakingly assembled six complete print-outs and had them finished and bound. To the uninitiated they looked like the real thing. These copies had been urgently air freighted from New York. Of course, Amy had been reassured by all that they would arrive on time. She had the tracking numbers; they were currently on Ascension Island (which was somewhere in the Atlantic). But counting up the days, she could see that there was very little leeway for mistakes. A grand opening without these crucial books would be a PR disaster. Walking to the window, she looked down at the snake-like river flowing through the city. Watching the ceaseless traffic of ferries, long-tails and bus boats, she wasn't totally impervious to a growing sense of foreboding.

Recognising a *Washington Post* food critic, Ken Rogerson, in the Author's Lounge of the Oriental Hotel and persuading him to host the book launch, brought some relief. She invited him to dinner to discuss plans. Corran, finally surfacing after his marathon sleep-in, joined them. Initially put out that Rogerson didn't actually know him, his restaurants or books, Corran suspected it was Amy he was really interested in. In reality, from bar girls to room maids, taxi drivers or crossdressers, Rogerson, a pathological flirt tried it on with everyone.

In his mid-forties, Rogerson, turning grey, loosing hair and worried about his shape, was working his way through a bitter divorce. Brought close to bankruptcy by a predatory horde of lawyers, accountants and settlement counsellors, he had abandoned New York for Asia. Bangkok, young, spirited, playful, had been the perfect getaway.

Amy talked up the glamour of the coming event. Since leaving university she had kept in close contact with several Thai friends. Many were working in Bangkok. Now influential professionals in the fashion and style press, Amy had been assured a heady mix of young models, stars, socialites and networkers, stoked into a frenzy of excitement by a rush of content from app-savvy bloggers, Instagrammers and Tweeters.

By the end of the week, these promises had come good. Several articles in the papers and online had featured the event. Her email box was filled with confirmations. The early trepidation that the day would arrive and only a trickle of liggers and free loaders would turn up, was replaced by a second, greater concern – she had over cooked it.

Five

Three hundred had been invited. But even before the rush hour had started, more than that number had swarmed into the lobby of the Carlton Wattana tower block and were berating security guards for entrance. Two hours later, staff at the reception desks, overwhelmed by conflicting guests lists, were already turning people away. The limited space of the Roof Terrace, not the best place to manage crowds, had already passed its recommended capacity. Even Corran, star of his own show and already late for several interviews, had been delayed in the foyer as the over-stressed reception staff fought to control the lengthening queues. Finally heading up in the elevator to the top floor, the doors had opened on a sea of faces Corran didn't recognise. With drinks free and the barmen clearly overzealous with their cocktail measures, an air of impending bedlam permeated the scene. Corran, casting his eye over the throng, didn't expect he'd ever find Amy, let alone the TV crew. But Rogerson he recognised, clutching a mojito, hogging the dance floor, a sweaty hand reaching out to hook unsuspecting girls. He looked younger: he must have dyed his hair and his teeth were supernaturally white.

Corran didn't have time to linger. Behind him a second set of lift doors opened, delivering yet another wave of eager party goers to the already crushed floor. As the new arrivals piled into the space, Corran was pushed deeper into the claustrophobic core of the crowd.

The music was from a Thai rock band. The lead singer, barefoot but wearing a tailored pin-striped suit, his wild blonde hair cut with fierce red streaks, was obviously well known; a close knit band of girls surrounded the main stage. When the chorus came around, they knew the lyrics and screamed out the words.

As the floor space filled up, many of the younger dancers moved to the tables and chairs to escape the crush. That was nothing unusual for Bangkok's social elite. But the fact that the tables were set just feet from waist-high glass screens, the only delicate barrier between them and the precipitous drop, added to the sense of decadence. Far from deterring people, the risk of falling only encouraged a rush for the edge. Smart phones lit up in the dark, as revellers out did each other to record more reckless selfies framed against a distant parking lot hundreds of feet below. In the pushing and shoving, plates and glasses were overturned. A couple began carelessly flicking cocktail fruit over the edge. Food soon followed.

Angry street vendors below, angered by the curious rain of tequila, Puglian olives and Tuscan proscuitto, called the police. No one turned up. Eventually two security guards, pressurised by the complaints from the street sellers, took the lift to the top floor. Fighting their way through the crowds, they attempted to persuade people away from the sides. Far from quelling the scene, their actions had the opposite effect. Out to taunt the agitated guards, more people surged into the space. A girl in a short sequinned dress was more provocative, twerking close to the edge. The leader of the security team, angered at being rebuffed, forced his way through the mass of people to pull the girl back from the barrier. But she was quick. He was only able to catch the end of her elaborate coral necklace, the delicate cable snapping in his clumsy grasp. Reaching out for the precious beads that flew out in a graceful arc over the drop, the girl unbalanced. A misplaced heel hooked through the straps of her designer handbag. She was lucky; although her foot flipped her bag over the side, she fell back into the arms of her shrieking entourage. Initially there was laughter, a momentary relief that was soon drowned by her hysterical screams. The reason came as a shock; it wasn't the bag she was agitated about (despite the brand label) – only minutes before her tiny pet terrier had taken refuge inside the main pocket. Pushing against her friends, the girl made a scramble back to the edge; it took four of them to haul her away from the barrier. Close to a breakdown, she was only eventually calmed when the missing toy dog was discovered under the table; cute furry face rammed into a plate of tuna crostini.

Amy saw none of this. Pacing the now empty lobby downstairs, her attention was locked on her mobile phone, the screen peppered with unreturned calls. Nine-thirty had passed and still the essential books hadn't turned up. It was an anxiety that had been on her radar since morning. A delay in customs had been the first hurdle. Assured that the packages had been cleared, she had sent a trusted assistant to personally pick them up from the airport. More than two hours ago he had sent a confident message that he had the special package in his hands and was close to the hotel. Since then, bizarrely, incredulously, frustratingly nothing. Why wasn't he taking her calls? It wasn't as if Bangkok wasn't one of the most connected cities in the East. Beads of sweat rolling down Amy's forehead and nose, began to despoil her appearance of steely, calm efficiency. Previously only a distant background hum, now a discernible, unsettling rumble within her core, the grim realisation that she was facing the first real disaster of her still nascent career, churned at her insides.

The call she yearned for finally came through. It was the courier. Stuck in traffic and walled in by buses and trucks, he was profusely apologetic; there was nothing he could do he calmly explained, "Welcome to Thailand, *mai ben rai*, chill, there is nothing can do." Amy screamed expletives, "Get out of the fucking car and run!"

Intimidation and threats are usually counter productive in Asia. Confronted with crude western-style aggression, Thais especially don't like to loose face; sullen inaction the likely default. Despite this, somehow it worked. Shocked by the sheer volume of Amy's outburst, the small man leapt from the air-conditioned comfort of the airport limousine onto the bridge. Choking on the diesel fumes and clouds of concrete dust drifting in from an adjacent building site, he staggered to the boot of the car. The package from New York was bulky and awkward without an obvious hand grip. He squeezed it under his arm and made a dash for the base of the ramp. The lights changed. Waves of scooters and motorbikes attacked from all sides. The limousine he was previously in, now freed from the congestion, sailed by into the far distance.

A quick glance at her watch told Amy that she couldn't delay any longer. Though it was an unpromising start – no books and no Corran – at least she could rely on Rogerson. Well known in high circles, once even appearing at the invitation-only TED talks in Vancouver, she knew he was a consummate speaker. But she was also slightly alarmed by how much he was drinking.

A prominent stage had been set up on a rostrum at the centre of the roof terrace. A towering enlargement of the book cover, *The Story of Food* looking like it had been chiselled in Biblical granite, dominated the impressive display. Four, under-lit, diamond-shaped blocks, specially constructed to hold the still missing volumes, looked all the more conspicuous by their emptiness.

Amy had the lights dimmed and the music turned down. Rogerson, balancing a delicate champagne glass on a speaker stack, took his time climbing the three modest treads to the microphone, each small step agonisingly laboured as if he were an Olympian about to receive a gold medal. Steadying himself on the side of the lectern, he started badly. Hesitant, muffled and subdued, his voice was difficult to hear above the constant background roar from the bar. When he twice referred to Bangkok as Beijing 'City of Angels' and kept leaning alarmingly to his right, those in the front looked concerned that he wasn't going to make it through to the end.

But Rogerson was just warming up. It was partly his style; a befuddled self-deprecation that showed that he was just being mischievous, toying with the crowd. More than proficient at public speaking, he rolled out the requisite anecdotes and witty asides, thankfully remembered the all-important sponsors and only marred an otherwise pitch-perfect performance by referring to Corran as Conrad. But again, perhaps he did that on purpose.

Rogerson celebrated the end of his speech by stepping down from the rostrum, wrapping his arm around Amy and coaxing her to the dance floor. Pushing him away, her evening was far from over. A message came through on her mobile; a text confirming that the assistant had arrived with the delivery from New York. A second read that he was on his way up.

Breaking a smile, Amy felt a wave of elation. The end of the ordeal was in sight. Her next big hurdle, her last big hurdle, was the presentation of these precious books to the ambassadors – elders from the houses of Diageo, Taittinger and Louis Vuitton. Out of the corner of her eye, she could see these grand dignitaries being ushered to their seats on the platform. Corran, author and star of the show, was the only missing piece of the puzzle. The obvious place was the kitchen.

Fighting her way back through the crowds, Amy headed to the foyer and took the lift down two floors. Parting the double doors at the end of the corridor, she could sense immediately there had been trouble. The kitchen was at a standstill. One member of the cooking team, pressing a kitchen towel to a bloody nose, was being consoled by his colleagues. On the floor in front of them a large tray of plates had been over turned. Amongst the broken china, seared asparagus grass, truffle leaves and soy-glazed sea kelp, floundered Australian Coffin Bay Oysters. To her right, a sticky line of black, like an agonised brush stroke from a Jackson Pollock painting, traced a tortured arc across the floor and the far wall: a kilogram of fresh beluga caviar, the black, silky eggs slowly sliding down the polished ceramic tiles.

But the greater shock was on the floor in front of her. A pile of torn pages, their edges uneven and ragged as if roughly hacked from a book with a butcher's blade, mixed with the remains of the rare and extravagant food. Bending to the floor she discovered the serrated words, 'Food', 'Story' and 'The', face down in the sticky, congealing sauces.

Six

Amy tracked Corran to a bar in the basement of the hotel. The 'Blackstar' was hidden at the end of a long corridor, so scuffed and worn it must have doubled as a goods entrance. Entering the dimly lit interior, she caught his reflection in an array of mirrored mosaics that covered the walls of the cavernous interior. The confused pixellated effect of the reflections, like a raw computer graphic, disoriented her. Although she could clearly see him, it took her a while to find his position within the maze.

Corran was sitting silently on a bar stool shaped like a laptop key, taking another drink from the ever-accommodating bar-girl.

Amy took the seat next to him.

"Where were you?" she asked.

He was surprised she had found him. Reaching for the bottle next to him – Mekong, a potent, but cheap Thai whisky – he ignored the question.

"You were meant to be doing the presentation."

"I didn't see the point."

"What do you mean? This was your evening, Corran, surely that's enough of a point?"

"You didn't see it?"

"See what?"

"The cover."

"What was wrong with the cover?"

"It was a goose. I told them to use the picture of the duck."

"What duck?" she groaned.

"The fucking Banbury Duck!"

That explained the torn pages.

"Aren't you going to pour me a drink" she replied.

Corran poured out a glass. She downed it in one. She didn't enjoy it. It was unpleasant, aggressive, its potency burning the back of her throat. But in the aftermath, lulled by the fierce punch of its raw alcohol, she felt strangely calm. Her anger and frustration, now defused, slunk back into the shadows.

When she had first come through the double doors into the seedy, tatty bar and seen him alone, hunched up at the front of the bar, her instincts were to lay into him, berate him, shame him for his dumb, stupid behaviour in shredding the books – "why hadn't he told her!', 'did he have any idea of the stress she was under, the hours she'd spent screaming at the couriers!"

But what use was it? It was done. It was over. To confront him now, with the best part of a bottle of crude Thai whisky marinating his already dark psyche, would only be inviting a duel with the devil.

She reached for a second glass.

Seven

It took Amy more than an hour and six strong espressos to coerce Corran back to the party – his party – on the rooftop terrace. Guiding him through the crowd, she thought it important that he show his face, mingle, chat – at least be courteous with the all-important networkers and bloggers. A 'no show' would only breed doubt and suspicion; malicious and dangerous gossip that the great show had gone off the rails. She also had deeper motives – important contacts that she wanted Corran to meet.

Andresen didn't look like a big-shot. Dressed in worn jeans, a faded, even moth-eaten T-shirt (can one manufacture moth bites?), he deliberately played down, some would say over-played down, any sign of riches or affluence afforded him by his hugely successful empires. A tatty Disney Swatch watch, given to him by a Syrian orphan in exchange for his mindlessly expensive Rolex, perfected the finer details.

Fresh from an afternoon's kite surfing on a beach in the Gulf of Siam, Andresen was regaling his audience with a description of a hazardous incident. A cord had torn from his harness. Momentarily losing control, he had been forced to vault the prow of an oncoming fishing boat to avoid getting run down. Having returned safely to the shore, he discovered a sea bass had caught in his harness; he must have hooked the fish as he skimmed the deck of the Thai trawler. Luckily for the world, he was wearing a GoPro on his helmet at the time. The incident was already racking up hits online.

Corran, still fighting the Thai whisky and oozing cynicism, had expected to hate this 'wealthier than Solomon', tech personality; it was rumoured he had once threatened a petulant patent lawyer by suspending him by his lapels above an ten-storey light-well. But on being introduced to the billionaire, Corran was taken aback by his unexpected charm and affability. Either the rumour mongers were wrong or Andresen had paid for some serious personality realignment.

Unlike the blunt and, in retrospect, oafish Rogerson, Andresen knew who Corran was. Along with dangerous sports and off-grid travel, he had wide interests, had read some of Corran's articles and even claimed to have tried one of his more unconventional recipes. Andresen was also up to speed with Corran's publishing deal with Font Lescari, having read about it in an entrepreneur blog. A blog, Corran later found out, his company owned. He'd come to Bangkok because he had wanted to expand in Southeast Asia; recruiting new people, programmers, producers and creatives. In fact, Andresen was just a regular guy, more regular even than a packet of Spearmint.

Favia, Andresen's South American girlfriend, blonde, beautiful, brilliant, and at times bashful, was also frustratingly difficult to dislike. A lecturer in Southeast Asian studies, she had used the opportunity of accompanying Andresen to the East, to take a tour with fellow academics of some of the more remote Khmer sites on the Thai-Cambodian border. Trained in archaeology and specialising in LiDAR satellite scanning of terrain, she was fascinated by unearthing the past; of seeing how even the simplest fragments might elucidate complex histories of culture and behaviour. Corran, bluffing it and knowing next to nothing about ancient Khmer history, had been rash enough to suggest that food was one of those factors. Favia agreed and acknowledged it was something she had overlooked and would redress. She typed out a reminder on her mobile.

While wanting to deride these moneyed leviathans, to find fault with their terrifying perfection, Corran, disarmed by their modesty and generosity could only muster something reluctantly close to admiration.

They got on well. The crowd of onlookers eventually died away, and the four found a quiet table away from the main party. Andresen had mentioned to Amy that he was flying north with part of his team to conclude their tour; rest and recreation at the end of a hard week's work. He suggested that Corran and Amy join them. Perhaps he could prepare a special gourmet/ideation experience for his people?

It was late when the party wound down. Andresen and Favia, exhausted after the day by the sea, didn't have far to go; they were staying in the hotel only two floors below. Rogerson, still pumped full of energy, wanted to continue on to another club. Corran and Amy politely declined. He went alone. Maybe that was always his intention.

Amy, taking a limousine from the reception at the base of the tower block, reminded Corran that he needed to be at the airport early for the flight north. She shouted the reminder twice across the carpark. He only half heard her.

Eight

Corran, edging the hire car out of the concealed underground carpark into the congested morning traffic, regretted his decision to drive almost immediately. Sukhumvit Road, one of the most tortuous roads in the capital, was a Herculean ordeal whatever the hour. With the street level cast into shadow by the bulk of the overhead Skytrain, the cracked pavements on both sides of the six-lane artery into the main city, were a netherworld of smokey food stands, cheap clothes stalls, flickering neon signs and confused telephone cables strung between concrete posts. The side streets were overrun with people hustling to work; office staff and uniformed school children, mixed with dazed backpackers and mangey stray dogs and cats.

Intense shafts of sunlight, cutting through the tall residential buildings, added to the already stifling heat. Corran reached for his sunglasses. Still bruised from the book launch fiasco of the night before, bitter episodes he'd rather forget played out like shadow theatre on the reflective glass of the newly-built blocks that surrounded him, the recall accentuated by a chorus of power drills.

A call from Amy had woken him early. Having spent most of the night speaking to the publishing team in New York, she was already at the airport. Of course, she was angry. But having witnessed how much Corran had drunk at the bar the night before, she'd already anticipated his likely morning state. She knew he'd fail to make the flight. Although she sounded pleasant enough – wishing him a cheery 'good morning', offering soothing sympathy for his seismic hangover – she was still a long way from forgiving him for the anguish and agony he'd caused her by taking a butcher's blade to the all important books. She was silently relieved to be travelling alone.

The car-crash of the evening had bought one small consolation. Font Lescari had acknowledged that it was their designer who had put the unfortunate goose on the cover. Amy had used the blunder to negotiate some crucial extra time for Corran from the previously intransigent executives. She had then put a knife to his schedule; publicity events in Singapore and HongKong were cancelled. With five clear days freed up, she had booked him into a remote retreat midway between Bangkok and Nong Khai, before they crossed into Laos and the old capital, Luang Prabang. It was to be a distraction-free break for Corran to concentrate on finishing his final chapters and getting the essential last changes to New York. Once processed they could finally hit the print button and put his bloated, petulant child to bed. On the 25th she would meet Corran at the hotel on the Mekong river.

Amy's plan looked perfect neatly framed within the aluminium margins of her laptop. But by the time Corran had fully absorbed the date changes and taken the taxi from his hotel to the car hire offices in Central Plaza (a round three hours), her well laid plans were already compromised. Wedged between pick-up trucks and decrepit buses, it took a further hour to crawl a painful five hundred metres to the first meaningful junction.

The reason was soon clear. A political protest had converged on the intersection. An angry crowd, sporting orange t-shirts and waving coloured flags, chanted and shouted out provocative slogans. A rudimentary stage had been set up at the apex of the crossing. Around this platform, folding steel chairs had been arranged in rows of ten. On both sides of the stage, ungainly speaker stacks had been roped to steel scaffold towers. A large blue canopy, stretched out over the seating area, provided the shade. A man with long bedraggled black hair tied back in a red bandana, was on the stage in front of a microphone. Curiously, it was a copy of the *International Herald Tribune* he was so gleefully shredding, that had caught the attention of the audience.

Catching sight of the distinctive IHT masthead reminded Corran that the lifestyle editor at the newspaper had promised to include a section of his Pacific beach tour in the travel and food supplement. Corran was pleased with the images – a red snapper grilled on an open fire on the beach, bedded on a salad of Wakame kelp and raw shrimps foraged from the rocky shallows (he even claimed to have caught the fish himself). Although the pictures had been sent, Corran couldn't recall if he had checked the final copy; alcohol still numbed his memory.

A shrill whistle blew. Seconds later a clenched fist landed on the boot of his hire car. He glanced up to see a traffic officer angrily gesturing for him to shift his car to the left; a gap in the crowd had opened up.

As he drove away, Corran glanced back at the stage. The newspaper was being set on fire. Still dazed from lack of sleep, he grew anxious, imagining that it was his red snapper and kelp salad review that was being torched on stage; his reputation and career in the hands of the fierce, jumping, dancing man.

Nine

Leaving the city behind, open countryside, palm trees and rice fields, flickered through the gaps between shop houses, tyre garages and factories. Crude wooden shelters with rusted corrugated roofs dotted the landscape. Buffalo drifted languidly along dusty tracks. An old scooter was in pieces under the shade of a bamboo grove surrounded by an array of tools. A mechanic, flat on his back, beer can locked in his grasp, was taking a nap.

In the middle of nowhere, a faux Greek mansion gleamed in the arid landscape. In the garden that surrounded it, an ornate Chinese bridge crossed a lake to an island. Much like a child's toy in a train layout, a miniature Dutch windmill and a Swiss clock tower had been neatly placed at the centre of a lush green lawn, so vivid it could only have been synthetic.

Sunlight glinted off the watery surface of newly irrigated paddy fields. A group of villagers, colourfully clothed, their faces shaded beneath wide-brimmed hats, waded knee deep through the sticky mud. Neat bundles of rice plants were being transplanted from nursery beds to deeper pools. Young and old, from small toddlers to aged grand parents, were helping out with the work.

In the central plains the majority of farmers planted jasmine rice. It was a popular strain, that bringing in almost twice the return, had gone on to conquer most of the dinner tables across the world. More than ten million tons made that journey from Thailand across the seven seas every year. Of course, Corran's tastes were more discerning. He used a less processed variety, brown jasmine, in his restaurants. Some of the rarer types, such as Red Cargo rice, recognisable by its deep purple, maroon colour, were so distinctive in flavour that he had featured them as dishes in their own right. In one recent recipe, he had infused grains in a subtle mix of sauces, spices and herbs and left them to marinade for twenty-four hours. The final dish, a single, tall tower of rice grains, surprised some by its apparent simplicity, even blandness. With no other ingredients on the plate, Corran had brazenly priced it higher than more sophisticated offerings on the menu. Yet the final taste, once savoured, had more richness and complexity than the rest of the courses combined.

From then on, rice had become one of Corran's private obsessions. At one stage, half crazed by the different varieties he was working with, the hasani from Iran, the nihonbare from Japan, the Nepalese pahele, Corran had put together a plan to open a chain of restaurants that served up nothing but rice. Starters, main courses, desserts, even drinks, would be presented in a range of inventive colours, textures and flavours. The restaurant interiors, designed to look like old colonial warehouses, with flickering gas lamps and raised timber walkways, would seat diners on hessian sacks around worn oak tables. Newspapers and menus were to be printed on rice paper, naturally, edible too.

Corran had started searching out expensive leases on the Sydney harbour front, when the investors, nervous at the scale of his ambitions, had pulled out. The plan was shelved. Though Corran hadn't totally wasted the knowledge he had gleaned. Rice and its four thousand varieties, went on to fill an entire chapter within his epic, 'The Story of Food'.

At the edge of the Khorat Plateau the road climbed into the hills. Limestone cliffs, jagged and majestic, lifted up like misty peaks in a Chinese watercolour painting. Storks nested in high trees. Deeper still in the forest there were monkeys. It looked wild, raw and poetic.

But almost as if the authorities had worried that the natural world might prove too unsettling to city minds, industrial tyranny soon returned with a vengeance. Appearing above the tree tops the ugly silhouette of a cement works cut through the smog. For miles on either side of the road, trees and vegetation were covered in a fine, dull brown dust. A security wall in front of the main installation had been decorated with murals. Painted by children from the local primary school, large balloon speech bubbles, decorated with colourful flowers and birds read, 'Nature and Harmony', 'Environment and Happiness', 'Prosperity in Concrete'.

Finally leaving the cement works behind, the road levelled out over open countryside. To his right, Corran could make out the steel, grey waters of the Takhang reservoir. At a popular viewpoint overlooking the lake, a line of tour coaches were unloading their passengers. Staggering down the thin steps of their buses, the weary travellers looked dazed to be out in the open. A family with four children, desperately searched the car park for a restroom. They made a panicked sprint across the hot tarmac to a low building in the shadow of the restaurant, only to encounter a queue that stretched round the block.

Corran turned his car into the carpark and found a covered space under the shade of a flame tree. A platform, built over the water, took in the full panorama of the reservoir framed on the right by a high plateau of distant hills. It provided the ideal photo opportunity for the tour group – the first on the long trip north. Couples, families, old and young, positioned themselves in virtually the same square metre of real-estate, took a single shot with their smart phones, before spreading out in search of the central attraction of the stop – buying savoury snacks and sugared drinks in the local market.

Years before, when there was only a single road heading towards the northeast, there were only a handful of stalls to serve the meagre traffic. Now with the road enlarged as a central artery to Isarn and beyond, the covered markets stretched out a full kilometre on both sides of the four-lane highway.

For Corran, these colourful markets at the confluence of so many provinces, were an opportunity to search out fresh, less-orthodox tastes. A constant flow of overloaded pick-up trucks, cars, and scooters, each with their own obscure local specialities, filled the stalls with sweets, fruits, dried meats and fish. Three times Corran returned to the boot of his hire car, arms filled with heavy bags and boxes of unfamiliar foods, some wrapped in leaves.

A bunch of scruffy kids drinking Coke and chewing gum, were bemused by the sight of a sweaty '*farang*' filling his car with so much of their archaic food. Out of playful curiosity they congregated around the boot of his Toyota and made fun of his choices. They began to get mischievous. Seeing his bags of fried locusts and grubs, they threw live cockroaches and beetles into the mix. To be rid of them Corran had to shell out several bags of Doritos and M&M's; not that he wanted them – they had come free with the rental.

After this diversion, (again, longer than he'd planned – it wasn't the only place he had stopped along the lengthy, highway supermarket), Corran found himself having to make up even more time. But the road was good, the traffic light, the only mild distractions, gigantic concrete dinosaurs, that craning their necks above the roadside palms, promoted distant palaeontology digs.

As the miles passed, anxieties about work inevitably invaded. Although relieved at the extra days Amy had secured to finish the last chapters, at the weekend he would be back on the PR bandwagon. A one-day gourmet workshop marked the end of the Thai promotions. For the intense eight-hour tuition sessions, Corran still had notes to write and recipes to prepare. If he felt adventurous, he'd make something up from the ingredients discovered in the roadside market. At one stall he had come across miniature mangoes no bigger than a plum; sweeter and more succulent than the famed Anwar Rataul from Uttar Pradesh, he'd never seen that in a dessert before. Then there was a thin stringy bean from the South – tender on the outside, incredibly bitter within. It would mix well with chilli and wild venison.

Fifty people had signed up for the tuition day. The majority were wealthy Americans or Europeans, most midway through retirement. He wasn't looking forward to the socialising, but the bed, the rest, the position of the luxury hotel on the banks of the lazy Mekong, would be a welcome reward to mark the end of what had become a particularly gruelling project; an incentive to get the last pages finished.

Focusing on this last hurdle, his mind flooded with minutiae; emails to send, headlines to refine, a catchy phrase for his speech. Reaching across the passenger seat for his jacket he groped for his mobile, thumb hovering over the 'speech' icon to dictate his thoughts. Sun flaring over the grubby screen made it impossible to read. Struggling to wipe the glass, Corran took his eyes off the road for too long. As the car lurched over the crest of a hill, a dark shadow fell across the screen. Snapping his attention back to the highway, Corran was shocked to see what appeared to be a giant haystack filling the road. He stamped on the brakes. The chassis of the small Toyota juddered as the ABS cut in and the tyres screamed to grip the uneven surface. But he was coming in too fast. There was an ugly dull thud and the sound of plastic splintering, as the front of his car disappeared under the muddy rear axle of a stationary truck. The engine stalled.

Ten

Corran stepped out of the car. Used to the air conditioning inside, nonetheless, he found it surprising cool. Alongside the road the dry leaves of a teak tree rattled in the breeze. Beyond, across an arid plain, dark clouds rolled over the far hillside. Sensing a change in the weather, he looked up as the last remaining rays of sunlight flickered and went out. Light rain started to fall, a soft humid mist that gave the road a slick, slippery sheen.

Walking round to the front of the hire car, Corran bent to examine the damage. It looked more alarming than it was. An indicator light was shattered and the bumper had been pushed up into the wheel arch. With no great effort, Corran was able to pull the cheap, deformed plastic away from the bodywork. If he brushed off the dirt, he could probably get away with it.

The Isuzu truck, its underside caked in layers of mud, rust and grease, was naturally untouched. The only noticeable casualty was a grimy child's teddy bear that had been roughy wired to the rear bumper – the collision had severed it neck and kicked the foam stuffing from its battered, sooty head.

Corran walked around the back of the ten wheeler. Cut sugar cane filled its two trailers. Peering down the incline searching for the cause of the holdup, wasn't encouraging. A long line of similar trucks, all overloaded with their own cargoes of cane, stretched far into the distance. Parked bumper to bumper, this long convoy looked like a single 'Great Wall' of sticks; a permanent feature of the landscape rather than one passing through.

Corran turned towards the cab. Loud rap music echoed from inside. Even before making the first modest steps to the front of the truck, he sensed that the sky had got darker. On the far horizon flashes of lighting were followed by an ominous rumble of thunder. Rain, previously only a light drizzle, suddenly fell hard. Seconds later, as if immersed under a power-shower, it became torrential,

Corran, midway to the door of the cab, stalled – it wasn't as if he needed to talk to the driver anyway; wasn't it just a small dent in an already battered bumper? And the teddy bear – he had it coming anyway.

Turning abruptly Corran made a dash back to the shelter of the Toyota. But his attempt to remain dry proved futile; by the time he was safely back inside, his shirt, trousers and hair were totally soaked. In the glovebox he found a box of tissues. Using them to wipe his face and neck he stared out. The unmoving bulk of the truck in front filled the screen, the red glow from its brake lights scattered by the hammering droplets.

Across the countryside the storm rolled in like a wave. The wind, howling over the fields, threw up dirt, sticks and leaves from the paths and tracks. A stray dog, hammered by the debris, scampered for cover. Palm branches, exposed to the full force of the deluge, bent double under the weight. A group of children, caught out in the open on their way back from school, took shelter beneath a tarpaulin stretched beneath the scaffolding of an advertising hoarding at the side of the road. Its bright, effervescent image of a super model in a red bikini, coolly sipping beer on a swing above a pool of half-man alligators, looked surreal and incongruous in the bleak surroundings.

A break in the clouds brought some hope. Momentarily a shaft of sunlight cut through the lower layers of funereal grey. Stabbing the ground like a burning lance, it blazed bright for seconds, flickered, then went out. There was to be no reprieve. The patch in the cloud closed over; a short, deceptive lull before a second, fiercer front rolled across the distant hills and began to gather momentum. Impossibly, the rain got heavier.

The harsh roar of diesel engines growling back into life, woke Corran with a start. Reaching for the keys he quickly restarted the car, as impatient horns sounded behind. Already the truck he had hit was someway down the road. Shifting the car into gear he accelerated to make up the distance. Several kilometres passed quickly, making it appear that the worst was over. But such optimism was brief. Lifting over a crest in the road, the now familiar rear end of the grubby Isuzu with its lacerated teddy bear, abruptly reappeared and he was forced to hit the brakes. Yet again he found himself sandwiched within the convoy of cane. Engines, both in front and behind, shuddered and fell silent.

This time there was a change of activity. As if on signal, a number of doors opened in the line of lorries. Their drivers, pulling on light plastic coats, stepped down from their cabs. Two men unrolled a canvas awning and tied it along the roof of one of their trailers. Others joined them. A small gas cooker was unearthed. An old cooking pot, dried noodles and some chicken cuts were found. Soon a potent soup was brewing. More metal stools and tables were squeezed under the crude canvas shelter. A bottle of spirits was uncorked. Another group brought out a guitar and a tin drum. Attracted by the first mournful chords, more drivers joined them. One of them had a trained macaw that appeared to nod its head in time with the music. In the flat monotone light, it took Corran a further ten minutes to realise it was a toy.

With the gathering fast turning into an impromptu street festival, Corran cast around for answers. A small pick-up truck passing on the far side suggested that the road south was still open. If he doubled back, he was sure to find another junction to Khorat.

Corran turned the car around and headed back down the far side. Some miles later he found a small sign leading off the main highway and turned off. He had no idea where it was heading. But with blind faith in his orientating skills and only too pleased to be free of the jam, Corran accelerated down the unknown country lane.

At first it looked as if his instincts were sound. The road, smooth and newly surfaced, ran parallel with the still congested highway. Seeing the tops of the marooned sugar cane trucks he felt some relief – smug even, that he hadn't surrendered to the lazy complacency of the drivers. And for several miles it looked like his good fortune would continue as he began passing the lead vehicles of the convoy.

Bright lights ahead brought more hope of deliverance. The comforting halo of a familiar Shell logo flickered through the palm trees together with neon symbols for a coffee shop and a restroom; a sure sign that reassuring civilisation lay just ahead.

Seconds later that hope was dashed. A roadwork sign flashed up bright in his headlights, as the track came to a sudden end. To his right a bulldozer and a tractor sat immobile. Banked up beside the machines lay freshly delivered gravel and sand. The materials that would have made it across the last fifteen metres to his salvation, the gleaming road-side garage, where a golden caramel frappaccino and cheese panini awaited in a spotless, glossy cafe. But to reach this oasis, Corran would have to traverse an ominous pool of oily black water, the approach marred by ugly rutted tracks. There was no way of telling how deep the mud was. In a powerful four-wheel drive truck it would be challenging. In his underpowered, front-wheel drive Toyota, insane. More demoralising still, beyond the low hedge he could see the previously deadlocked convoy starting to move off.

Frustratingly, Corran was forced to turn around again. But driving back, it was soon clear that he was going south once more away from the highway junction. Blanking out the obvious logic he pressed on.

It got darker. The density of overhanging branches shielding the road from the light, didn't help. And as the foliage got thicker the surroundings became bleaker, more menacing. Rain, pounding relentlessly on the roof and windscreen of the car, sometimes obscured the worn tarmac entirely.

Corran switched the lights to full beam. A tractor coming back from the fields surprised him. Its six occupants, clutching a pot-bellied pig across their laps, had wrapped themselves in a ragged PVC sheet. Huddled together on the wooden bench seat, they didn't even register how close they'd come to a fatal collision.

Coming over a rise, Corran soon found the hoped for crossroads. But a single signpost, cracked at its base and bent over at an angle, was so stained with age the directions were unreadable. The road directly ahead, water logged and strewn with broken, twisted branches, didn't look promising. And the track to the right led only to a dead end and what appeared to be the locked gates of a private plantation. His only option was left.

As the road climbed steeply through dense forest, the conditions further deteriorated. Large chunks of the tarmac had broken away entirely, marring the surface with dark pools of reddish-brown water. Through bamboo groves that skirted the winding track, Corran could make out the corrugated iron roofs of small shelters nestled in the undergrowth. One group of shacks, so weather-worn and squalid, were tied together with old rags and torn shopping bags. Between two of the most wretched huts, a string had been stretched. It looked like dead rats had been hung out to dry, although from such a distance they could have been any small animal – dogs, maybe cats.

Crossing the crest of the hill, the winding road descended through a thin cutting into a gorge. An old timber bridge spanned an angry river, the water so turbulent that waves occasionally washed over the rough hewn planks. Corran hesitated. While some of tue wooden spans seemed robust enough, they were also broken and rotten in places. Several sections had even been removed for repair.

Shifting into a low gear, Corran cautiously edged the car onto the first half of the bridge. The force of the torrent, rising up over the side of the boards, gently rocked the small hatchback from side to side like a toy in a bath. Half-way across, a loud thud on the rear passenger door was unsettling; it must have been a log borne along by the current.

Eventually Corran reached the far side and coaxed the spluttering Toyota up a slippery slope away from the river. He was relieved; the crossing had been been far worse than he had expected – no way was he going back.

Now some distance from the valley, Corran scanned the landscape for signs of life, hope or habitation. He needed to find out where he was, ask directions, hopefully call Amy. Dim lights from distant huts flickered through the trees, but nothing suggested the outskirts of a village, let alone a town. He checked his mobile; the signal remained weak.

Despondent now, Corran struggled on, condensation starting to cloud the windscreen. He put the palm of his hand up to the glass to wipe away the moisture when suddenly a large shape flashed up bright in the beams. In Corran's already fevered imagination, it looked like a small child falling through the air, its arms spread out wide like the wings of a giant bird bracing itself for the coming impact. There was an ugly, loud crash. Corran instinctively lifted his arms to his face thinking that the glass would shatter. Whatever it was struck the windscreen and bounced off. With a certain dread, Corran looked back over his shoulder, expecting to see some struggle, some agonised movement from limbs that were crushed by the collision – there was nothing, just a lifeless palm branch lying in the road.

Of course it was nothing, but the shock had badly shaken him. The tension had had him scream out; a series of crude expletives blaming the hire company, the Thai nation, and Jose Mourinho, in no discernible order. He was also getting tired; any lingering confidence that he was going to escape from his gloomy labyrinth by trial and error had long since evaporated.

Slowing the car, Corran turned off the road and pulled up on a sandy bank. He peeled his fingers from the steering wheel leaving deep nail indentations in the leatherette padding. Turning off the engine, he let his head drop to his hands.

He thought of Amy. She'd be there now; probably lying by some exotic infinity pool shaded by palms. His mind filled with regrets;

why hadn't he just listened to her and taken the earlier flight? Vanity was the only dispiriting answer. If this was retribution he probably deserved it, a yellow card for hubris handed down by some pious moral referee. Inwardly he laughed at the idea that some form of karmic payback followed our transgressions. Who even had the time to police such futile misdemeanours? Heavenly hosts? You'd need heavenly technocrats. All seeing ones. Millions of them, with clip boards, pencils and night vision goggles.

A piercing whistle some way off in the woods stilled his childish ramblings. He looked out through the windscreen; the weather had cleared. Rain, that had ceaselessly hammered the body of the car, was now eerily quiet. Like curtains pulling open on a pantomime show, the clouds parted; low shafts of sunlight cut through the trees.

As the heat returned, steam lifted off the now glistening road surface. Better still, the break in the weather afforded Corran a view through the dripping undergrowth to some rooftops close by. He could make out the glow of hanging lanterns. It looked like a small cafe, perhaps even a restaurant. Suddenly he felt thirsty; he could get a drink, ask directions, hopefully find food. Reaching for his jacket and mobile, he got out of the car and took a track in the direction of the lights.

Eleven

A rough track wound through grass and damp undergrowth. Steps, half hidden in creeping vines, climbed onto a raised platform. Around a clearing in the still dripping trees, half a dozen tables and chairs were laid out. A balcony was built out over a small, gloomy lake.

Thinking back on that moment several days later, Corran couldn't understand why he hadn't simply turned around and returned to the car. The place was decrepit, even a touch creepy. Everywhere he looked there were signs of neglect and decay. The floorboards, still waterlogged from the storm, were cracked and rotten. Tired and faded lampshades swung from overhead branches. Small ceramic figurines, stained by years of harsh climate, sheltered in miserable alcoves. Shrivelled, half-dead plants, hung limp from cracked earthenware pots. A single electrical cable, winding through low bushes, led across a walkway to a rough timber building that must have been the main kitchen, its corrugated roof patched with sheet metal from an old real estate hoarding. All should have acted as subliminal signposts sending him back down the track to the car.

Corran had turned to take in the view from the balcony, when he heard movement from the main house. A girl appeared in a doorway. Long black hair, falling over her forehead, partly hid her features. Only when a gust of wind blew in across the surface of the lake was the veil momentarily lifted. Her face was curiously pale, round and dumpy; forehead creased in a frown as if perpetually pained. Eyes, dull, languid, suddenly flared like glowing coals in a fire, as she focused on him with unsettling, almost animal intensity. Before he had seen those eyes, Corran had no intention of staying. But her look, her presence – so unbearably close to him – exerted an uncomfortable influence.

Finding a chair on the edge of the balcony he sat down. It was a damp position, awkward and constricting. A table leg had recently been replaced on its frame giving the surface an irritating imbalance. Conscious that he was the only one there, Corran picked up a sticky, frayed folder and opened it. The menu, typed out in a large Thai font, filled four pages. Someone with a dying black biro had scratched out most of the food entries. Sellotaped additions had been crudely stuck over many of those that remained.

Corran glanced back at the steps he had come up. He toyed with the idea of making a run for it. He could be down the steps and back in the car before she'd even noticed he'd gone. Even if he was intercepted he could make up some flimsy excuse. Being a *farang*, better still, a lost, ignorant *farang*, explained a multitude of sins. His mind was racing towards such an action, his arm already reaching for the edge of his chair, when suddenly he sensed her back at his side. Trapped, he'd have to order something. Quickly scanning the pages of foreign script, he found the one symbol he could understand.

"I'll just have a coke," he muttered, tapping the page.

The girl scribbled a note in her pad. He thought it would be enough, that the order would satisfy her, but to his annoyance she remained implacably at his side.

Reluctantly Corran picked up the menu again. He pointed randomly, carelessly to two prominent lines on the menu (a bold, playful font), probably the specials. With no idea what they were, he did it to get rid of her; he had no intention of eating it. This time it worked: she softly took the menu from his hands – he thought he even detected a smile – and returned to the kitchen.

Left alone and adjusting to the low light, Corran had time to take in the full horror of the place. The platform on which he sat looked out over a small, dreary lagoon. Nearer to the main shack a thin wooden boat was tied up. Half-submerged in the murky, muddy waters of the lake, the canoe hadn't been drained for months, possibly years. An oar and a plastic bowl floated in its prow. Looking out further across the water, Corran thought it unusual to see the dead headlights of a car peeking up from the depths. He knew his cars. It was even a recent model. He was thinking through the rationale of how such a thing could have ended up in the middle of the lagoon – it was a long way out for an accident, even if the car had jumped from the main road – when there was a sound from the kitchen block. The waitress reappeared. Drinks came first; his coke (in an old vintage glass bottle – he hadn't seen that for a while) and a small accompanying jug of water with ice that had almost melted. He was pouring out the coke when she returned with a larger tray filled with two dishes. These she slid onto the table without any due care or diligence, then headed back across the bridge to the shack.

Corran drank the coke quickly; he was more thirsty than he'd thought. But the meal he ignored, left untouched. It was what he had expected – bland in appearance, uninviting, devoid of any artistry (it was tragedies such as this that had first inspired him to become a chef). And the speed with which it had been delivered hardly lifted his confidence. In his mind's eye, he envisaged the girl, impatient to be home, scooping up spoonfuls from a pre-warmed vat and dumping two inelegant piles on the dish. She obviously knew little about presentation; sauces had seeped over the side. The plate had also been positioned so that the rice faced towards him – and the rice itself, the most fundamental of cooking skills (especially in Asia), hadn't even been drained properly; the grains oozed with gooey starch.

Corran turned the dish around and leaned closer. It didn't smell of much. Maybe the still lingering scent of damp was too intrusive. A small bowl of prawn crackers had also come with the meal. They were probably from a packet. These he quickly finished. But rather than satisfying his hunger they left him wanting more.

Reaching for a fork, he examined the dish. To the side of the rice there were vegetables and some kind of meat. By its texture alone he couldn't work out whether it was chicken, pork or fish, although the species was probably the least of his concerns. Wily to village cuisine, he suspected cheap animal cuts – tripe, stomach linings, lungs, bulking up the mix. He had seen such a bucket hidden under the counter in less reputable markets. The prongs of his fork pierced a piece of something. Slippery and rubbery in texture, he sniffed it, then childishly flicked it off the table. The meat bounced off the railings, cleared the bushes and fell into the dark inky waters beyond. There was a loud splash. Something big devoured it. It could have been a fish, a big fish, but a fleeting glimpse of something resembling a scaly tail (caught in the last glow from the sun) suggested something reptilian. Corran thought of dumping the whole plate into the lagoon, but given that what ever it was had made such a kerfuffle over a single small bite, a plateful would have attracted his mates (and his mates might be larger). Besides, although he couldn't see the girl, he was sure she was watching him. The door wasn't open, but there was a side window on the wall facing him covered with a mosquito screen, behind which she could safely remain unseen.

Against all better judgement, his fork fell again to the plate. The realisation that he hadn't eaten for hours, combined with the unease that she might be crouched behind the thin gauze, finally forced him to try a mouthful. Starting with the rice he gradually mixed in some sauce and swallowed. The first two spoons didn't register. He was starving and his actions were purely perfunctory. Only by the third bite did the full impact of what he was tasting break through his ennui. It was as if whole ranks of taste buds, that slumped like forlorn girls on the rejects bench at a school dance, had finally come alive. A wave of sensations, starting from the tip of his tongue then moving to the back of his mouth, fused into a single powerful current that surged through his frame. His first reaction was one of shock, incredulity. Looking back down at the plate, a seismic gulf lay between the expectations of what he was eating and the extraordinary flavours he was experiencing.

Corran put the fork down and paused. He felt confused, unbalanced. Suspicions and doubts crept in. Had he missed something? Was some cruel hoax being played? He cast around, half expecting to find that his reality had changed, that he wasn't there at all, but lay instead within the comforting embrace of a Michelin-starred haven, surrounded by glowing chandeliers and supercilious sommeliers. It wasn't so. The harsh reality returned: cheap, shabby lampshades, grubby table cloths and the uncomfortable sensation of chair splinters inching through his jeans.

There was a second explanation. His state of mind might have been a cause. The drive through the rain had over-stressed him – latent hunger and thirst caused an overreaction. Hadn't desert survivors described brackish water as being like the finest Champagne?

Armed with scepticism, his attention returned to the dish. He took another, larger mouthful and chewed slowly with more thought and deliberation, ready to be critical, itching to find fault. But his suspicions were unfounded; a second wave of flavours, more powerful and distinct than the first, quickly killed any wavering doubts. With hesitancy displaced by lust, he surrendered to these impulses, letting the intensity of these feelings swarm into his consciousness.

These were not the vivid revelations that one reads about from seers, shamans and soothsayers, of mystical creatures, winged fish and effervescent angels: there was no altered state, no 'out of body experience'. His reaction was physical, chemical; a chorus of synapses and neurones all crowding and jostling for primacy, their exuberance betrayed in a kaleidoscopic stream of colour and light.

And then there was quiet; a great stillness.

Beads of sweat had broken out across his forehead. Reaching across for a thin paper napkin, Corran wiped his face. The action of cooling his forehead brought momentary relief; time to recalibrate his thoughts, regain some much needed equilibrium. With his emotions in check, he forced his mind to focus on the technical minutiae, the ingredients and fine details within the dish.

Clearly there was lemongrass, coriander, garlic, roasted chilli, and a sweetener, probably tamarind or palm sugar. But then there was the unknown, something intangible, mysterious, difficult to unravel. Somewhere, hiding between the folds of very ordinary fried beans, bamboo shoots and herbs, lurked an enigma he could not explain. Like a chemist scrutinising a petri dish for a hidden catalyst, he combed through every element on the plate, but could find nothing of worth or meaning.

There are meals in one's life that are worth the price and agony of a long-haul flight. Experiences so vibrant and resonant in memory that they are etched in life histories for ever. The concept of Grand Cuisine aimed for such lofty ambitions. Treating culinary events like opera, every element was elevated and enhanced to a new level of sophistication and refinement. From the ambience of the dining room, to the small details and touches – the arrangement of the place-settings, the colour and texture of the napkins, the temperature of the wines, the smiles of the waiters and the dresses of the waitresses – all was orchestrated and stage managed with faultless precision. Discipline, detail, discernment – that was the creed. Perfections that touched every psychological base: sight, touch, smell and sound.

Here there was nothing.

Corran woke from his reverie to find that hours seemed to have passed. He starred down at the dish in front of him, now wiped spotlessly clean. His face was smeared. At some point he must have pressed the plate close to his face and, like some grubby alley cat, licked the last residue from its surface. But despite such demeaning behaviour he remained baffled. Hidden and obscured within the deceptively simple food he had just eaten, something pure, unadulterated still escaped him. And behind that secret there had to be some craft, there had to be a cook. Of course, it could be the girl. But judging from her appearance – she was thin, delicate, probably too young to have the depth of experience – he thought it unlikely. Someone else was in the kitchen. It had to be a member of her family, an elder sister, father or mother; maybe it was someone older – a great aunt, even a grandmother.

Corran turned around. With the sun well below the horizon, the light had changed. This time he could see through the thin mosquito net into the glum interior of the building. There was no one there. For the moment he was sure he was alone. He glanced across at the front and the back of the shack. Both were clear. The worn wooden door at the entrance didn't even look like it had a latch; it would be easy to get inside.

Silently Corran stood up and walked away from the table. Pausing momentarily at the railings over the lake, he pretended to take in the view. Seconds later he crossed the small bridge over the lagoon and stopped in front of the kitchen block. He listened. It was quiet. Stepping gingerly up to the window, he peered inside.

The kitchen was surprisingly stark. A heavy wooden chopping block, looking like it had been crudely hewn with an axe, served as a main preparation table. Not that there was anything being prepared. The surface was wiped clean. A frayed hose dripped into a worn plastic bowl. In it he could make out his plate – the plate he'd shamefully licked clean – and his cutlery (also spotless). In the corner of the room a hot charcoal stove balanced on a rough stone plinth looked like the only cooking point. Wooden shelves around the room were almost bare. There was the odd cardboard box, a jar of dried herbs, a tin tray with rusty screws and a spanner and a plastic carrier bag holding a scuffed motorcycle helmet.

The longer Corran starred at the space, the more perplexed he became; how such threadbare surroundings could have produced the meal he had just eaten mystified him.

Curious to know more, he lightly pushed against the door handle. Despite old rusted hinges it swung open abruptly. Suddenly she stood in front of him. With her hair washed and tied back he could fully see her face. Earlier he must have misjudged her: she was unsettlingly, dangerously beautiful; an attractiveness, that like a supernatural force, seemed to suck the breath from his lungs, sapping his confidence. Of course, he should say something; apologise, explain why he was there, make up some lame excuse about looking for the bathroom, or waffle on about how he was well-known, famous (as if fame explained such transgressions). But her piercing golden eyes, fixing him like a mountain lynx sizing up a field mouse, rendered him pathetically silent.

Five minutes later, Corran had crawled back to the hire car. Painfully he reflected on those few seconds; why he had failed to speak to her, his ignominious retreat, the excruciating embarrassment of handing her payment for a meal that was way more than generous. But above all, it was his failure; his inability to discover the secret of the kitchen that riled him most. Its value for the book was immeasurable. He was there – so frustratingly close. Why couldn't he have been more dogged, more persistent? At the Hiro San, he'd taken on a small army of armed gangsters. Reckless, sure, but he hadn't come away so miserably empty handed.

But there was something else – something about her, something that had wrong footed him. A vitality, an aura, an unsettling energy that had multiplied his confusion and rendered him helpless. The recollection of this weakness made him squirm. A discomfort that rather than causing him to meekly accept defeat, only reignited his anger. It wasn't over. He had to go back, confront her, convince her, coerce her with money, anything – he had to get the recipe.

Corran snatched at the buckle of his seatbelt. Kicking open the car door, he walked purposefully back through the long grass down the track towards the steps. He climbed the treads rapidly, two at a time, ready to cross the veranda to the door of the shack. But reaching the top of the platform, he found the place in total and utter darkness.

That in itself wouldn't normally have been enough to deter him. He had never been afraid of the dark – as a child he often took walks in the dead of night. But a cacophony of alien noise – loud cicadas, a particularly unsettling shriek from a bird of prey high in the trees, and the slippery sounds from whatever languished in the gloomy lagoon – was slowly undermining his resolve. A third dimension invaded his fears; somewhere, close by, whether from the shadow of the shack, or the bushes to the side, he imagined she was still watching him.

Twelve

Chaiyaphum, a small town a hundred and fifty miles south of Khon Kaen, put its name on the map because of a single market product – it produced and sold the popular and spicy Isarn sausage, *sai krok isarn*. Corran had chanced on the place simply because after leaving the restaurant on the lake, he had blindly driven straight. And Chaiyaphum was at the end of that line.

Arriving late in the evening, he had mechanically booked into the first hotel on the first corner of the first street – the Namsai Golden Resort. Built in the late eighties in the then fashionable post-modern, Asian style, it had hoped to attract the tourist traffic to the area's only major cultural attraction, the modest stack of stones known as Mor Hin Khao. No Angkor, it was otherwise known, in lightly mocking tones, as Thailand's Stonehenge.

The hotel had exploited this neolithic theme. As an expensive publicity stunt, three monumental limestone slabs were positioned as an arch in the simple foyer in imitation of the ground portico of the ancient site. But when large cracks had opened up in the basement laundry room, construction engineers declared the building unsafe. In the ensuing fiasco, a large section of the roof had to be removed, to allow access for the cranes to lift out the blocks. With a negative press ridiculing the inflated plastic stones that replaced them, any remaining goodwill towards the hotel understandably died and the promised tourist hordes never materialised.

The manager of the hotel, in a desperate bid to rebalance the books, transformed the Namsai from the travel trade to business use. The large garden restaurant was turned into a conference centre and the basement into a karaoke club and internet hub – "wifi with bargirls".

It was only by accident that the hotel found favour with a second, unrealised demographic – travelling salesman, those peddling western lifestyles, fridges, air-conditioners, TVs and PCs to the former communist republic of Laos. Purely by virtue of its geography, the Namsai was exactly (to the last inch they claimed), equidistant between Vientiane and the centre of Bangkok. An ancient milestone was "discovered" on the outskirts of town. This proud monument went on to replace the miserable and rather deflated stones that had previously gathered dust in the entrance hall.

Even though Corran hadn't drunk anything the night before, he woke with a dull, hollow emptiness; a gnawing unease that his small, previously unassailable empire of one had unravelled. Something had gone badly wrong. It was as if his whole purpose, all his hopes, aims and ambitions, had been derailed and, like boxcars crushed together after a terrible collision, now lay twisted and immobile at the bottom of a forgotten chasm.

He surveyed the room. Though he had only occupied it for less than six hours, it was a mess. Both his cases were open on the floor. Clothes had been thrown over the sofa and chairs. The contents of his washing bag littered the tiled bathroom floor. For some reason he must have taken out the latest proofs of his book. Page spreads covered the coffee table, reading desk and the end of the bed. With a thick red marker he had written cryptic remarks over large sections of the text. Yellow stick it notes had been stuck between chapters. Some sections had been torn in half, the uneven tears betraying his impatience. And the fall out – a wastepaper basket filled with crushed pages.

A hotel writing pad near to the bed revealed deeper anguish, its sheets scrawled with crude sketches and diagrams. Corran was no artist. The fierce, overworked images reflected his futile attempts to jolt his memory – rekindle some crucial, perhaps overlooked detail, from the night before.

Corran grabbed a T-shirt and trousers and pulling them on, crossed the room to drag back the curtains. Sunlight punched into the room. Shading his eyes from the angry glare, he looked outside. A team of contractors was in the garden erecting a stage and laying out tables and chairs. The Namsai was hosting a Texan cowboy convention. T-bone steaks, corn cobs and imported craft beers, were on the menu. A poster, featuring Buffalo Bill and Pocohantas in a clinging embrace, announced a generous prize for the best-dressed Wild West couple. Electricians were testing the sound system. A wall of brutal black speakers punched out sudden bursts of country and western. Such a blast had obviously woken him.

Corran turned away from the window and walked to the door. It opened onto a dark corridor. He reached for his bulky room key. A lightbulb on the landing had gone out and not been replaced. It made it difficult to see. But as the door scrapped open across the uneven tiles, the piercing sound triggered a fleeting memory from the previous evening. As if projected onto the murky canvas of the corridor, he saw the haunting outline of the girl framed by the doorway. Her look, the clarity of her eyes, her hair, were already indelibly scarred in his mind. But this time, a small, almost imperceptible detail that had previously alluded him, crept from the shadows. Half-hidden within the folds of her long dress she was holding a knife. No ordinary cutting knife, it was a heavy chopping blade, the kind that butchers use to cleave large carcasses.

The faulty light bulb on the landing flickered on again. Corran blinked with the brightness. Though the image from his memory was lost, its imprint stayed with him as he slowly walked down the stairs. By the time he had reached the hotel foyer, with the noises and sounds of the day intruding, its potency had faded; only the lingering outline of her face, her hand and the icy, blue reflection off the tip of the blade, remained.

Thirteen

Dao Pramot, the deputy manager of the Namsai Golden Resort, had served loyally and efficiently at the hotel for more than twenty years. He had trained in Bangkok as a waiter and barman at a small hotel sandwiched between the cafe's and clubs of the notorious backpacker district, Khao San Road.

Dao, always eager to help out beyond his official duties, ran errands, booked cars, recommended restaurants, even devoted entire evenings to entertaining guests with tours of some of the more unusual nightime attractions. Popular with the guests, he rose quickly to a position as food and beverage manager. And save for an unfortunate incident, he would most probably have stayed there.

At a farewell drinks party for a tour group of beauticians from Stockholm, a middle-aged woman had made a damaging accusation. Money had gone missing from her make-up case. It wasn't a lot. A little short of $50. But she had accused Dao. He had been in the room at the time of the incident retuning her DVD player. She wanted to have the staff rooms searched. The management, swayed by gossip that Dao had a gambling addiction, had persuaded the woman not to involve the police by paying the amount in full. Dao, infuriated that this had in effect constituted an admittance of his guilt, had left suddenly under a cloud. Besides, his mother had been ill with a heart condition. Relocating to Khorat to take care of the old woman and his two younger sisters, had been the ostensible reason he had left.

The owners of the Namsai, still struggling to reinvent themselves after the fiasco with the foyer monument, had been only too pleased to have someone with such knowledge and experience joining them from the city. And, although the hotel had never really pushed above average for anything other than its enviable position at the entrance of town, Dao, remembering his hotel management seminars, had given the Namsai a single unassailable difference to keep his TripAdvisor rating in positive territory. He had created the best breakfast buffet in town. Forty-nine international tastes, both European and Asian, crowded the menu. A towering display of tea was on display, together with fifteen choices of coffee, including the luxurious Sumatran *kopi luwak* (made from coffee beans refined from the droppings of the Asian palm civet).

In small-town Chaiyaphum, such grand gestures made headline news. It was a reputation that even the newly-opened International in Khon Kaen, lorded over by an impressive line-up of suave Swiss managers and fussy French chefs, couldn't compete with.

Dao's ability to dream up such an enviable breakfast spread had come from his Bangkok days. Exposure to a cosmopolitan mix of French, English, Japanese and Americans, each with their own distinct and often petty demands, had both baffled and intrigued him. Finding such produce in Bangkok had been difficult enough. But sourcing the same menu in remote Isarn had needed the probing instincts of a detective.

A Belgian, who had taken up a position at the university in Khorat, had a wife who had opened a small bakery. She supplied cup cakes, Danish pastries, croissants, brioches, and Dao's current favourite, passion fruit macaroons. An Italian engineer, seconded to a hydroelectric plant and home sick for his local food, had located producers who could make cured meats and a 'mozzarella-like' semi-soft cheese (they had got away with goat's milk). A retired Japanese businessman had even mastered the art of *tamagoyaki*, having borrowed a recipe from an aunt in Narai.

Initially that was the plan: global tastes from four continents, but ensuring the produce was locally grown, fresh, ethical and hopefully, organic. The managers made a big deal of it in the promotions. A large banner across the hotel frontage featured colourful snaps of beaming villagers in straw hats driving their baskets of lush vegetables and fruits to market on buffalo-drawn carts – even the cattle looked healthy and fulfilled.

In reality, given the punishing hours, the gruelling schedules and the unreliability of his suppliers, Dao got lazy. A Tesco Lotus (a joint enterprise with the British supermarket chain) had recently opened between Khorat and Khon Kaen. Disdainful of their brash, gleaming new premises, Dao had gone there to mock the whole vulgar arrogance of it all. But a quick glance at the well-ordered, softly-lit aisles only confirmed the futility of his 'buy local' endeavours. It was all there – fresher, cleaner, better packaged, for less than half price. With sleek new trolleys with super-smooth castors, it would take less than half an hour to load up with everything he needed.

Only too happy to wave goodbye to the mafia of petulant farmers who haggled incessantly over their stunted lettuce and misshapen fruit, Dao discarded his precious contact book in the conveniently sited recycling bins and filled up his trolley.

No one seemed to notice the change. Of course, the cheery village promotions, maintaining the impression that everything was 'local', eco and pure, stayed the same. And the switch, quietly phased in over a month, never made an impact on the revenues. Businessmen and salesman, often with their second wives, even second families in tow, ensured that the tables were always full and frequently justified a second sitting. To Dao personally there was a third, greater benefit. His budget remained the same. He could pocket the not inconsiderable difference.

Coming down late, Corran was minutes away from missing Dao's culinary showcase. A seasoned business traveller, he had breakfasted at some of the world's most salubrious tables. Although no one could touch Jeffrey Ming's six-finger breakfast at the Elan in San Fransisco (which included gravity-defying poached eggs slowly baked in revolving currents of super-heated steam), Corran was still impressed by the sophistication of Dao's offering; a pleasant surprise in such a provincial backwater. He found a large plate, and like anyone still dazed with mid-morning lethargy, overloaded it with far more than he could finish.

Leaving the breakfast room, Corran took the doors into the garden. He found a remote table away from the pool area, already filling with noisy kids, and a long way from the cowboy stage now starting to resemble an over sized-wigwam.

Identified by hand-written cards, Corran had taken all of the house recommendations – a papaya, mango and star fruit salad, a selection of miniature croissants and Danish pastries, which warm to the touch appeared to have been baked on site, followed by some soft cheeses and what appeared to be aged Tyrolean speck.

It all looked good on the plate, the pastries crisp and flakey, the fruit especially fresh. But despite its undoubted allure, he found he couldn't touch any of it. His appetite wasn't the problem; he'd never knowingly missed a meal, even out of illness. It was a deeper unease that inhibited him – haunted by his experiences of the night before, he had a dread, of course irrational, that even something as innocuous as bread or fruit, might smother his recollections of the extraordinary flavours that still smouldered in his memory.

Going against his own exacting standards of personal hygiene, he had even failed to brush his teeth the night before, acting much like a lovelorn school boy, struggling to retain the sensations of a first stolen kiss from the captain of the hockey team.

A particularly brutal burst of drum and bass from the sound stage cut in. Other, more intrusive sounds, invaded; a child who had fallen by the edge of the pool and cut his forehead, was screaming for his mother. At an adjacent table, a particularly vocal businessman was ranting at a waiter who had forgotten his order.

Before he had sat down, Corran had ordered a double espresso. The waitress, new, was anxious to please. The machine had just broken down. When offered a plain cafetière, his look of disappointment had been so profound as to send the distraught girl scampering into town. An American coffee franchise had opened on the crossroads at the centre of the high-street. She caught a lift with an off-duty security guard. The round trip had taken less than ten minutes. But by the time the girl had returned triumphant to his table in the garden, Corran had already gone – his mountain of food untouched, except by the flies.

At the top of the stairs Corran's mobile rang. He knew it was Amy. Glancing at the screen he saw that he had already missed several calls. He cut the call. Wise to his tricks, she called back almost immediately. Taking a deep breath he answered.

She was concerned. They had booked a conference call with Chris Stratton to discuss the troublesome goose cover. He had missed it.

"I called four times. You didn't get my messages?"

"I must have over-slept..."

"Where did you sleep?"

"Someplace off the main highway."

"Where?"

"A small town, Chaiyaphum."

"You didn't make it to the Agora?"

"There was too much traffic."

"You called to cancel?"

"I got in too late."

"I really stuck my neck out to get you in there, Corran. For a reason. To work. I didn't do it to have you taking joyrides."

"It wasn't a joyride, Amy."

"What then?"

"I can't get into that right now."

He was hiding something.

"Right now's good. I'd rather know now."

"I need to make changes."

"What kind of changes?" she asked, full of suspicion.

"Another chapter."

"A chapter?"

"Six pages. That's all I need."

"Two days from the deadline, a deadline you've already shifted five times, you haven't a chance."

"I came across this place, in the middle of nowhere. It changes everything."

"You said that about Moroni, you said that about the Hiro San."

"This is way beyond both of those. It's that special, that unique..."

Special, unique, the words seemed so tame, so inadequate to express the extraordinary. Of course she was right, he'd said that before; such currency was debased. It had never occurred to him that he might chance upon the real thing.

"So, you want me to call Lescari?", said Amy breaking the silence.

"Yes."

She sighed; it was futile arguing – she'd be making the call anyway.

"I'll do it Corran. I don't want to. Because I know exactly what they're going to say..."

"What?"

"They're going to say No Fucking Way!"

There was a pause. Amy regretted the expletive.

"If that's what they say, tell them from me, without the changes, I'm not doing it."

He'd said it calmly without anger or bitterness; a bluntness of tone that alarmed her. Before he'd always left room for manoeuvre, a door left slightly ajar for compromise, for discussion to show he respected her judgement. This time it was different. There was a hint of irrationality, even foolishness, she hadn't experienced before. What the hell was he doing? He was prepared to push everything, the whole fragile edifice, four years of painful work, over the edge. Why would he do that? For what? Something petty he happened to chance upon in the night?

She felt her neck stiffen – a headache wasn't far away. Of course she should be forceful, put an end to his madness. But she could sense a whole train load of emotional metaphors ready to roll down the line if she tried. Too early for a confrontation, she lost courage. And she had more immediate concerns – a hotel full of guests on a gourmet cooking weekend waiting impatiently for their promised celebrity chef. She weakened.

"I'll make the call," she groaned.

"Thanks Amy. I'll be there. I promise."

"Look," she cut in, "I know this is the last thing you want to talk about..."

She was right; it was the last thing he wanted to talk about – the Gourmet Weekend. Partly his fault, he should have cancelled it. Three thousand a head had something to do with it, their healthy deposits already cashed. And no one could have foreseen that the book would still be crowding the schedule.

"I'll be there," he repeated.

Corran put away his mobile; he'd survived the call and bought a small window of opportunity. He turned for the door. Cleaners had already been in the bedroom. It took him a while to find his camera bag. This time he wouldn't take any chances. He had two cameras – a high-resolution Nikon D3X for the main shots and a compact Leica for small details. A wide angle and a macro lens added to the line-up. Back-up batteries, two lighting stands, a tripod and a silvered reflector were also packed. He wanted a good portrait of the girl; her sultry looks were sure to add tension and intrigue to otherwise static shots of food. Grabbing a jacket and his notebook from the bedside table, he headed for the door and the stairs to the main foyer.

Walking past the reception reminded him to get money (he'd spent more than he thought at the roadside market). The cashier didn't have enough in his cash till. A call was made for the accountant to open the safe in the back office. Sixty thousand baht was counted out on the desk top. It was a lot. He hoped he wouldn't need it; though he was sure to use the remainder on the rest of the journey north.

Around the side of the reception desk, Corran chanced on a small book shop. He picked out a detailed terrain map, probably ex-military, and walked to the cash till. Two women were behind the counter. Paying for the map, he described the restaurant, its position in the trees and the view over the lake. They were confident that they knew the place. Corran unwrapped his map. Although initially confused by the symbols and colour coding, the two women ended up pointing to two completely different locations within the grids.

Dao, overhearing the conversation in the manager's office next door, came into the shop and offered to help. Corran repeated the description. Dismissing both of the girls' suggestions, Dao came up with a third possible location, decisively tapping his index finger in the opposite corner of the map.

Outside in the corridor, Corran could see other staff converging on the small kiosk, primed with their own input; it was hopeless. Patiently thanking them all for their suggestions, he folded the map, collected his change and left for the carpark.

Dao, coming out from a trade entrance, beat him out onto the forecourt.

"Ban Kai is where you should be heading. It's close to my mother's house."

He was going in that direction anyway. A staff meeting had been cancelled. He had some time. Knowing the area, he offered to drive. When they found the place, he could also act as an interpreter.

Fourteen

Dao's pick-up was decrepit. At some point it must have been involved in some fatal accident. From a distance, its chassis appeared bent, as if two different cars had been crudely welded together from two halves. But though battered on the outside, the interior was disturbingly clean; the red, faux leather seats so obsessively polished they were as shiny as a kitchen counter. Only a crude line of bolts, where the door column met the floor, spoiled the impression of harmony.

It was the small details that intrigued Corran; the bronze lucky amulets hanging from the mirror stalk, the neat row of windscreen stickers from country clubs and gun shows, a framed photograph of a local TV star with a heart drawn in fuchsia lipstick (supposedly hers), over the scuffed cellophane cover. More disturbingly, on the floor of an otherwise spotless cabin, there was a semi-translucent sheath that looked ominously like a snake skin.

"It was from the pool-house," Dao cheerfully explained. "They shed their skin every six months. It's what all the screaming was about earlier."

He reached for his car keys and turned on the ignition.

"We killed the mother. A banded krait. Very venomous. They think there are still baby ones hiding in the croquet set."

Corran thought back to the breakfast; the noisy kids running mindlessly around the concrete cartoon characters standing in the long grass; maybe not the safest playground...

Dao forced the gearstick into first and the car lurched urgently forward. If the twelve-year old pick-up was in bad shape, Dao's driving was yet more disturbing. Due to some freak engineering defect with the differential, Dao's foot was either flat on the accelerator or hard on the brakes. As the truck leapt through the hotel entrance into the mid-morning traffic, taxis, a small bus, a tuk-tuk overladen with newly fired pots, all braked and served to accommodate them. Angry horns sounded. The tuk-tuk driver, close to over turning, shook his fist and, uncharacteristically for a Thai, screamed shocking expletives. Corran, embarrassingly visible on the passenger side, weakly lifted his hand as a small gesture of apology; but it did little to soothe the fury of the shaken man. Dao, again on the accelerator, and making for an impossibly thin gap in the outside lane, appeared oblivious to the chaos and distress he had caused.

Although Chaiyaphum was a small town of no more than fifty thousand, the density of vehicles within its streets was unusual, as if the entire population was on the move at exactly the same time. The worn leaf springs of the Isuzu creaked and groaned, as Dao, weaving between buses, small pick-ups and scooters, took shortcuts through the thin alleys and side streets. Corran was relieved when a last turn through the service block of a hospital saw them back on the ring road. They headed south.

Dao knew the road well. It was dry and the weather had cleared. Following Corran's description, it didn't take him long to find the point at which he had driven off the main highway the day before. In the morning light, the billboard featuring the beer-drinking model and the clamouring man-crocodiles looked taller, more garish, its vast bulk casting into shadow the stunted paddy fields behind.

Once onto the country tracks their pace slowed. The rhythm of the engine, previously erratic and unbalanced, also calmed. It was something to do with the petrol mixture, explained Dao; to save money he often topped up with chip oil from the kitchen.

So that explained the smell of fish and chips, thought Corran, opening the window to clear the air as he took in the passing scenery.

At first little looked familiar; it took time to align his turbulent memories from the night before with the calmer scenes they were now passing through. In the dark, the incessant rain and wind had produced a tunnel like claustrophobia, shaped by the dense overhead foliage and accentuated by the feeble headlights of his struggling hire car. Now, bright sunlight, cutting through the thick canopy of trees, revealed a totally different world of verdant, regimented fields and well-tended orchards stretching across the rambling hills.

A small house, recognisable by its brightly-coloured tiled steps, brought the first comforting clue. Further on, Corran remembered an old spirit house wrapped in the gnarled roots of a banyan tree. From then on familiar sights became more frequent. He felt relieved. They were clearly on the right road.

At some point, he reached into the back of the car for his camera bag. He perched it on his lap, wrapping the strap around his shoulder, in anticipation of reaching the location. As soon as the car had stopped, he wanted to be out of the cab, his equipment ready, to head down the grass track to the veranda. To reenter the kitchen was his primary concern. Somehow he had to get past the girl. The memory of how she had wrongfooted him still rankled. This time, clear in his mind as to what he needed to achieve, he wouldn't allow himself to flounder about like some dazed adolescent.

Once she was tamed, Dao could help with translation. He needed to establish whether it really was her, or some stashed-away grandmother who was the real talent, the craft. Then he needed to extract the crucial information, to check if any special methods or techniques had been used. More urgently he wanted to get his hands on the ingredients, the key spices, herbs and sauces. He'd even brought along some small self-sealing boxes to collect and preserve them.

In his mind, Corran planned through the additional shots and pages he would need to produce. The opening spread, a wide-angle shot, would be from the track. Early morning mist would have been useful, but it was already late. Dao could always light some damp foliage; he'd noticed a cigarette lighter in the side pocket of the door. Rather than recording its bleak reality, the sad desolation of the place, he wanted to create an air of mystery and enchantment. Vines and branches could be positioned in the foreground of his lens to suggest a sense of something precious that had been lost and was now rediscovered – naturally by himself, the intrepid gastronaut.

From there on, the job would be more prosaic. He would need the stock shots of every restaurant review; the wide angle of the veranda and the lake (the production team could photoshop out the unsightly cars), and the quirky details to add texture and intrigue to the piece – the worn carvings, the faded lanterns and the plants that thrived despite the neglect. All this would build up to the highlight of the chapter – beautifully composed shots of the food on some pure white dishes (he'd been wise enough to take some from his hotel room). These he would take on the main deck. Considering the brightness of the midday sun, he would have to use both reflectors, even a back light. Though he didn't want anything that was too over stylised; he wasn't after Conde Nast Traveller gloss – the images needed spontaneity, authenticity.

After the food he would deal with the girl. A shot of them together might be worth the effort; if he could coerce a smile out of her icy, dour looks.

With any luck he'd be finished, packed up and on the road north in two hours. He was a fast driver. If he was stopped (as so often happened when he was in Thailand), at least he had ample reserves to bribe the police.

The truck turned around the corner of a hill. Seconds later the familiar crossroads came into view with its distinctive bent sign post. The route to the bridge and the river was to the left. Corran raised his hand in anticipation of reaching the junction and was on the brink of pointing out the turn, when he suddenly froze. Somehow it didn't look right. The signpost was wrong, the main support a different colour. Corran hesitated. It can't have been red, bright vermillion red? The truck sailed on. Seconds later he was having doubts. Turning in his seat he looked back over his shoulder.

"I think we should have gone left," said Corran.

"Left? Where?"

"Back at the junction."

Dao braked and stopped the car.

"You're sure about that?"

"I think so. Yes."

"I know that road. Driven it many times. Just past the hill there's a big sugarcane factory. You can see the sign for it. The whole area has been burnt and cleared. No trees. Is that what you remembered?"

Corran stalled. He looked behind him again. There were obvious landmarks he clearly remembered; a broken wooden fence and a small circle of blackened tree stumps. But there were also details that looked completely alien: a bulky container on ungainly breeze blocks – surely he would have remembered something as obvious as a concrete water tower?

Ahead there was a second junction. It looked similar. He dithered. A pick-up truck sounded its horn behind them.

"Well?" asked Dao calmly, in no hurry to move despite the shadow of the truck looming ever closer in his rear mirror.

"Give me a second".

Corran got out of the car and walked down the road. Dao was right about the sign. Its headline was even in English: 'KSL Group, PLC, Sugar Processing Plant', with the sub text in Thai. He'd made a mistake. Walking back up the incline, he got back in the car.

"You want me to go back?" asked Dao, hand reaching for the reverse gear.

"No, I was wrong," replied Corran eventually.

"You look unsure. Really, it will only..."

"No Dao, you know the area. You're clearly right. It must be the next turning."

Dao drove on. Corran looked ahead to the next junction. Yes, he must have got confused. This was the correct turning. It was easy to make a mistake. Indeed, the weather-beaten signpost, buckled at its base, looked almost exactly like the first.

Fifteen

By midday they were still on the road. Every corner, every group of palm trees, every spirit house, weather-worn teak house and mud-splattered buffalo, looked familiar yet so wrong. Corran had been obsessive, questioning each turn, direction change or deviation. Dao, who likely had hundreds of his own errands and meetings to attend to back at the hotel, took every instruction and reversal without complaint or reproach, coaxing his struggling pick-up down rutted, overgrown tracks and unmarked roads, cutting through villages that weren't even on the map. It had got them nowhere.

Optimism soured to despondency. Every call that came through on Dao's mobile (evidence that he was indeed a busy man), had Corran nervously checking on his own. New York would be waking in a few hours. Amy's email reporting on their earlier conversation would be making unwelcome breakfast reading. Wasting time on his fruitless treasure hunt was hardly improving his status.

Dao stopped the truck at a small stall selling grilled spicy chicken. A group of rice-growers were boiling husks of sweetcorn over a charcoal fire. Dao used the opportunity to question them. The map was unfolded on the grass. Once again everyone struggled to understand the complex contours and symbols. Dao patiently orientated them by showing them the location of their own village in relation to the newly-opened Tesco's on the main highway north. Several spoke with an air of great authority and made excited, decisive gestures across the dry landscape, yet no one had the remotest idea of any lake, let alone a restaurant.

Dao, not wanting to appear ungrateful for their help, bought several chicken skewers and cans of Pepsi from the street stall. It came with a crude *som tam*, a spicy vegetable salad prepared by an old woman by the side of the road, absent-mindedly hacking through a basket of papaya with a brutal machete. The chunks of papaya, coarse and uneven, were mixed with snake beans, dried shrimp, chilli and garlic. Thrown together with almost deliberate haste it looked a bit of a mess. Yet the balance of sweetness, sourness, saltiness and heat (critical to the taste of one of Thailand's most renowned dishes), was captured with almost lab-like precision. The old crone had obviously been honing her skills all her life. Her nonchalance was a sham.

Corran and Dao sat on the tailgate of the now dusty Isuzu and chewed their modest lunch in silence. Returning the empty Pepsi cans to the seller, Dao wanted to banter with the villagers, but Corran, pacing restlessly up and down the grass verge, made it clear that he was too agitated to stall any longer.

Soon they were back in the pick-up. The search area widened to take in Nong Bao in the south and Wat Huai in the east. They even passed the notorious tourist attraction of Mor Hin Khao. Since they were there, Dao suggested a detour to visit the place. Corran reluctantly acquiesced. Dao thought the short walk to the site might raise his spirits. It had the opposite effect; Corran's impatience to be back in the car only darkened his already temperamental state.

Despite this Dao persevered. He found a local guide asleep in a visitors' centre. The dazed official, shocked to have rare clients at the monument, was more than happy to give them the tour – the extended circuit. Following a path through uncut grass, he enthusiastically pointed out the unusual shapes within the rock formations; there were giant elephants, a family of turtles, and, if you really unleashed your powers of imagination, a tall sailing boat with four masts.

Corran, feeling the heat and unable to concentrate, could see none of these things.

The guide suggested an additional walk to some more remote formations that included a set of prehistoric cave paintings further up the hill. The man claimed to have unearthed fragments of a neolithic meal preserved in the shell of a rough earthenware vessel. Dao readily agreed, but turning around found that Corran had already left them. Looking down the hill they saw him leaning over the bonnet of the pick-up, pouring yet again over the well-worn map.

Back in the car, they continued. More signposts were followed, tracks driven, landscapes traversed. Soon Dao had pretty much exhausted every road he knew in the area.

Coming across a hill-top monastery, they chanced upon a Buddhist monk. The man in his mid-sixties, wore large orange shades, curiously without lenses and padded headphones missing their lead; he must have picked them up in a store stocked with products without purpose (maybe his own personal reflection on the redundancy of technology).

The monk showed them his quarters – a six-foot hole cut in the limestone cliff. Apart from his shades and headphones, a begging bowl and a toothbrush were his sole possessions. This time it was Dao who showed impatience. Corran, swayed purely by the fact that he spoke competent English, wanted to question the monk about the restaurant. Dao gestured that he thought this futile. Corran persisted. His instincts were right. The man knew the place. It wasn't far. He was able to give explicit, step-by-step instructions that no one could get wrong.

"By the bridge, it's easy, over the hill, you can see it a mile off."

"If we can get to the bridge, I can find it myself," added Corran, remembering his struggles over the river.

Leaving the monastery, Dao was immediately dismissive, suggesting that the man had been drinking.

"I wouldn't trust him ... if you know what I mean", said Dao, purposefully swaying as if dizzy with alcohol.

"How can you say that?", asked Corran, affronted on the monk's behalf.

"Under his blanket, I noticed a whisky bottle."

"What if he just used it for drinking water?"

"And outside by the rubbish tip, ten bottles more."

Nevertheless the directions were followed. After driving for a further half an hour down a thin precarious track along an arid river bed, a building did appear as predicted. It turned out to be a Mexican-style hacienda, standing alone in the middle of a pineapple grove. Although a small fishpond was indeed filled with Koi carp, dispiritingly it didn't look remotely like Corran's muddy lagoon.

The owner of the smallholding had once worked in a fruit-canning factory in Minnesota. Nostalgic for middle America, he had built the diner to complement a worn-out sixties' Ford Thunderbird he was struggling to restore. It was in bad shape. Someone had wired a set of cow horns to the grill. The car's seats, torn from the interior, were eerily occupied by a family of shop mannequins, their heads holed by shotgun pellets. Broken washing machines and second-hand fridges littered the grass verges. They didn't stay long – the dusty arena was home to a pack of malevolent dogs, using an open deep-freeze as a guardhouse.

The setback brought more disappointment. As the sun dropped below the trees, shafts of golden light flickered through the palm groves, casting long, thin silhouettes of workers returning home on their bikes. The beauty of the scene, enough to excite the eyes of the weariest of travellers, did nothing to break Corran's gloom. Even Dao, previously confident that it was just a matter of time before they found the place, grew increasingly despondent as the light fell. The energy, the hope, the urgency, had all gone.

To lift the mood Dao switched on the radio. A local folk band was playing. It was a catchy, spirited tune. Dao, tapping his fingers on the dashboard, whistled along. But Corran, with his eyes still locked to the road, was past listening. Not that anything made any sense to him anymore; everything passed in a confused, amorphous blur, as if they were driving around in circles, the sameness of it all needling his sanity.

What had gone wrong? It should have been easy, simple to find. He could have been in the place, found the moody girl, taken the photos, nailed the ingredients and had it all wrapped up and off to New York before Callister's team had even woken. Designed, printed and bound, it would all have been over. This rarest of discoveries, this extraordinary thing, this secret recipe, would then have been his.

The car slowed to a crawl then pulled up by the side of the road. Dao, switching off the engine, turned to Corran. He looked pensive.

"I think I might have made a mistake..."

"What do you mean?"

"We might have been looking in the wrong place," Dao answered, his voice tremulous, almost confessional.

"How?"

"Well, your starting point has always been the big ad. The poster of the beer girl?"

"So?"

"There's more than one, Corran. They're all over the place. On most of the main roads around here."

Dao reached for the map, now creased and folded in all of the wrong places.

"When you left Bangkok, which road did you take, where was it signposted?"

"It makes a difference?"

"It makes a big difference. There are two highways past Chaiyaphum. The west towards Phetchabun and the east towards Khon Kaen."

"It was Phetcha Bunn, I think." Corran replied, finding it difficult to pronounce the name.

Dao reached for a packet of chewing gum, took a piece, then handed it across to Corran.

"That's what's been worrying me. I think we've been searching on the wrong side of town."

"You sure?"

"I'm certain. I live here. I should have known better."

A second, more significant insight hit him.

"Worse than that, I think I've been really dumb."

Shaking his head he sighed.

"... you have to forgive me," again the contrite tone.

"Forgive you for what?" Dao looked so forlorn, so disconsolate it was beginning to irritate him.

"I know the place. I've been going there for years."

Sixteen

Half an hour later, Dao slowed the Isuzu, turned off the road and parked up on a grassy bank.

"This is it," he announced triumphantly. He turned off the ignition and reached for the door.

The high-pitched squeal of the pick-up's rusty door hinges breaking open woke Corran. Blurry-eyed, it took him a while to take in his new surroundings. Although he can only have dozed off for less than ten minutes, it seemed like an eternity, his dreams heavy with rich, extravagant detail. Waking from the profound sleep, left him groggy, out of kilter. A deep red mark was etched across the side of his cheek where his face had fallen against the seat belt strap. Through the murky windscreen, smeared with a day's worth of dead bugs, he could make out Dao already midway down a track, energetically waving for him to join him. Dutifully he left the car and followed, stumbling over the uneven path, his mind still dead to any sensory input. The surrounding trees and undergrowth passed by making little impression. It looked different from his recollection – but the light conditions (it was earlier than before) could have accounted for the changes in similarity.

It was only once he had caught up with Dao and taken in the full ambience of the place, the scent of the damp grass, the irregular whine of the incessant cicadas and the rustle of leaves in the trees, that his lingering doubts began to ease.

More concrete clues were starting to fall into place. He brushed by a flowering vine. Seeing a similar plant the night before had made him think back to the harbour-front park in Sydney; in the botanical gardens there were several climbing the walls. Thick spider webs that stretched between the branches of low bushes (watched over by their disturbingly large sentinels), also matched his memory. A piercing scream overhead reminded him of the large bird that had so spooked him before.

They approached the steps. The worn treads looked familiar as did the sticky touch of the half rotten banister rail. Climbing up onto the terrace, he took in the view over the lake. Its veranda was laid out with the same number of tables and chairs, the rough floorboards dotted with identical weather-beaten gnomes and cracked pots.

Corran allowed himself to get excited; a boat, half-submerged by the water's edge was exactly as he remembered it. And amongst the faded water lilies in the lagoon, he could make out the familiar shape of a car bonnet protruding through the mire; surely not every premises was in the habit of dumping cars in the lake? It had a Japanese badge, a Mazda. That didn't add up. He might have got that wrong.

Corran was ruminating on these vexing discrepancies, when a door opened on the kitchen building across the bridge. A waitress appeared. Incredibly, in appearance, by hair colour, her complexion, the shape of her dress, she looked exactly like the girl he'd been hunting for. The shock froze Corran mid-step. Still dazed from his abrupt sleep, he had trouble coordinating his wits, fully engaging his senses. He was sweating; he could feel the beads breaking out across his forehead.

Crossing the bridge, the girl came towards him. Corran timidly backed up against the railings to allow her more space. As the waitress passed by, her tray heavy with bowls and plates, he focused in on her face – her eyes, her hair, the nuances of her expression – all the small details that would either confirm or deny a match. In that split second his hopes brutally evaporated: it wasn't her – so clearly wasn't her; the difference ludicrous, laughable.

Yes, she was beautiful. As were her two companions working tables on the far side. But there was none of the magic or mystery that had so bewitched him just twenty-four hours before.

From then on everything looked, more than wrong, deceitful. The boards of the veranda weren't wood but tiled, the tables were covered with a fussy floral veneer, the chair squabs, plastic, not cane. The illusion of isolation and remoteness was in turn displaced by more intrusive sounds he hadn't noticed before; a busy highway could be heard just beyond the line of trees, ten-wheeled trucks roaring by on both sides. At the entrance gates, beer crates were being noisily unloaded from a delivery van. And from the kitchen a chef with an irritatingly shrill voice screamed at his staff.

For Corran, this altered state came as a crushing blow. It was like watching a stage show come down after a spectacular performance, all the ropes, pulleys and stays, more than destroying an illusion, mocking one's gullibility for believing.

In his impatience to be away, he made for the steps. Dao's voice stalled him. He looked across the floor. The hotel manager, merrily smiling, was waving to attract his attention. The man had managed to secure a table in a good position overlooking the water. Raising a cupped hand to his mouth, he signalled that he had already ordered drinks. This vexed Corran. No way could they stop now. It would only waste time. The light was failing. If they were to have any last chance of finding his place before dark, he had to keep Dao driving.

Corran crossed the veranda to cajole Dao back to the pick-up. He was midway to the table when the drinks arrived. Dao, perhaps anticipating what was on Corran's mind (he could sense his irritability a mile off), launched himself at the nearest beer. Pointing to the empty chair next to him, he drained the glass. As Corran reluctantly sat, Dao reached for a second. The drink went down more rapidly than the first. Corran winced; he'd never get the man back behind the wheel now. He was a bad enough driver without being drunk. But then again, thought

Corran, in a moment of rare solicitude, why the hell should he? The man had given up his entire day to drive him around; he was rightly exhausted. At a petrol station in the afternoon when he had filled up his tank, Corran had offered to pay. Dao, treating him as his guest, had refused. The least he could do now was buy the man a drink (drinks he mentally corrected). And then, once he was satisfied, possibly infused within a bath of black coffee, coerce him back on the road.

"This is it?" asked Dao, triumphantly. "This is the place? The restaurant, the lake? You don't want to take any photographs?"

Corran, not wanting to crush his enthusiasm, forced a smile.

"Yes... It might be..."

"Wait a moment? 'Might be'. What is this 'might be'?"

"Look, I'm certain it is Dao. I just want to be completely sure..."

"Oh, I know what you mean, yeah I know, I know. It's the food. Only the food matters. Ok, ok. That's what you want, we try it, then you'll see," Dao reassured him.

Protest was useless. Corran was forced to go along with the charade. A waitress was called. Like the first girl, she too was playful and pretty. A conversation was struck up. In any language it was obvious that Dao was shamelessly flirting with her. They giggled over a joke. Glancing across at Corran, she looked coy, flashed her eyelashes and chewed the end of her biro like a bashful schoolgirl. Dao, obviously pleased with himself, leaned closer to Corran.

"You see..."

"See what?" muttered Corran, still snappy and on edge.

"She said she remembered you," he grinned mischievously.

"She's sure?" asked Corran sceptically.

"Yes, she's sure. She recognised your camera bag."

Of course, Corran hadn't taken his camera bag. If he had, he would have finished the whole damned business there and then and they wouldn't be sitting where they were wasting time. Instead, he would have been hundreds of miles away, relaxing in a five star retreat on the banks of the Mekong river sinking back more exotic cocktails than the pitiful selection he could see populating some of the adjoining tables.

"Let's order," announced Dao.

He opened the menu. Flicking through the pages, he pointed to various entries and gave some hurried instructions to the waitress. The girl, closing her notepad, looked surprised. Only after she had disappeared did Corran realise the full import of what had just been imparted.

"I've ordered everything on the menu. All the starters, main courses, even desserts. We can pick and choose the best bits. Soups, spicy curries, fish, prawn, crab, chicken, beef and pork. That way, you'll be sure to find the dishes that got you so excited."

Corran inwardly groaned, the chances of a quick getaway melting away. With six pages to the menu (two of which were filled with chef specials), it was going to be a gruelling ordeal. And, alarmingly, there were only two of them. Either Dao was being exceptionally generous or he had already secretly deduced Corran's true status (it would only have taken two clicks on Google) and surmised that 'the world famous chef' would most likely be picking up the bill.

Of course he should have been frank to begin with; come clean, tactfully broken the news that Dao's venue, nice that it was, wasn't remotely like the real place. But looking at the man, clearly in high spirits and convinced that his ingenuity alone had heroically solved Corran's cryptic quest, he didn't have the heart or the courage to disabuse him.

More drinks arrived. Dao, before he had even touched his lips to the fresh glass, ordered another. He drank a lot for a small man. Corran, in contrast, sipped his drink slowly. Contemplating the hotel manager over the rim of his glass, he could see the man's movements becoming languid and lazy; beady eyes gleaming like neons in a back alley. One more litre and it would all be over; Dao would be catatonic, unable to stand, let alone drive. Why fight it, he asked himself. Surely he should just surrender, accept his fate, give up and relax?

Looking over the lake, despite the obvious waste and litter, there was even some poetry. As the setting sun sliced through the low cloud in a blaze of crimson, bright orange ripples spread out across the surface of the water. Amongst the reeds at the edge of the lagoon, colourful dragonflies danced over the water lilies, their delicate gossamer wings catching the last dying light.

Getting lyrical, Dao expounded on the joys of living in a small provincial town close to the country. He had been more than happy to turn his back on the stress and chaos of grubby, polluted, Bangkok. He recounted his travails as a hotel deputy. And although Corran sensed some unmentioned drama was responsible for the speed of his sudden exit from the metropolis, Dao never touched on the incident with the Swedish beauty therapist. He claimed that it had been his plan all along to return to Chaiyaphum when he had made enough money. It was where he was from. The move put him closer to his infirm mother and his two younger sisters. The girls were sweet but totally useless when it came to looking after old people. Of course he had been concerned that after the excitement and sophistication of the capital, he would find life dull and slow in such a comparative 'backwater'. But he liked the intimacy and the spirit of community he found in the villages. In good times and especially bad, there was a sense of solidarity and shared destiny. People were close and stayed together. Ok, there was no big culture, no glamorous shopping malls, or large arena shows by famous international pop bands. Yes, he missed the creative buzz, although he did hang out with a number of local musicians and artists, who had been able to scrape together a reasonable living by doing their own thing. And as for the 'fame' thing, he had a special eye for young talent at the local *luk tung* festival. Isarn was well-known for feeding the Bangkok fame machine with fresh new faces – he had a producer contact on a TV chat-show at Channel Seven, who gave him a finder's fee.

Strangely, despite never really being a spiritual person, he had also got more religious. Near Khao Nok there was a monk who was very respected by the villagers. Even wealthy Bangkokians made the five-hour journey to attend his talks and sermons. They also brought money and donations to support a glitzy new temple build – flatscreen

TVs, iPads and Samsung air-conditioning units were now the accepted currency for good karma and a comfortable afterlife.

"Temples in Bangkok are boring, mainly funerals. There's no fun down there. Here ceremonies are more colourful. People meet to gossip, play music and especially eat. The Buddhist stuff is ok. But there are other things that watch over us. People in these parts are superstitious. The spirit world lives and watches over them. Good guardians to protect and, if you don't behave, bad ones to haunt. Taking on ghostly form, they live in trees, rivers, old houses and for the unfortunate few, the loos. They can also fly. Sometimes late at night in the middle of nowhere, when you're alone, it does get a bit freaky."

Dao finished his beer. He paused before continuing.

"You saw the big arch at the entrance of the town?"

"Showing the tourist sites?"

"Yes, the incredibly famous spicy sausage, basket weaving and the usual pictures of Mor Hin Khao. Well there's a fourth image people never notice."

"The big vegetable thing."

"It's known as the Witch plant. It really stinks. Beetles like it. It catches bugs in its sticky leaves and kills them. They say that in the depths of the forest there are giant ones. Big enough to wrap themselves around a child. An uncle in my family said he nearly lost his boy of six. He had strayed into the forest. The voice of a girl had called out his name. The boy had wandered too far and fallen asleep in a clearing. Hours later he woke to find himself being suffocated by leaves that were slowly strangling his neck. He was lucky that a villager, out shooting birds, heard his screams and was able to tear him out of the branches."

Killer plants – that was weird. There was a silence. Dao took a long deep drink. With his eyes wondering erratically over the tables and inevitably settling on the the pretty waitresses, he was now dangerously tanked.

Corran had time to reflect on his story. It was an awkward tale. He wasn't sure if he should dismiss the narrative or be spooked by it.

Was Dao trying to unsettle him? Was it a warning that his own quest was down to forces he didn't understand, that he was trespassing on cultures that weren't his own? Was Dao suggesting that he was the victim of a similar entrancement?

Corran's mobile rang. Standing to answer it, he muttered an apology. Dao didn't need it; with his arm wrapped around the waist of a passing girl, he was already distracted.

It was Amy.

Seventeen

"They won't go for it Corran," said Amy.

"You told them how important..."

"It was just 'no'. Didn't even want to discuss it."

"Twenty-four hours. One more day. That's all..."

"They don't want to know. The deadline is set. They won't move it."

"I want you to get back on the phone. I want you to..."

She cut him short.

"You're fucking this up, Corran. Why?"

Her tone had been surprisingly belligerent – out of character even. The line went dead as Corran cut short the call.

She should have expected such a reaction; she'd clearly been out of line. But she was hot, irritable and fed-up with shovelling up a constant mudslide of problems that Corran was so obviously self-manufacturing. It was over, done, finished. Why delay? For god's sake, wrap it, print it, ship it!

In truth, Corran's exasperating wanderings had had more serious repercussions; Amy had only just survived a second, taxing day with sixteen, high-maintenance V.I.P. guests, on the first leg of their 'Southeast Asian Gastro Experience'. Fresh off a river cruise from the old Lao capital, the select few had been in a state of excitement at the prospect of meeting their world-famous chef.

So far Amy's lame excuses and explanations for his delay had been accepted with good grace. But she wasn't so slow to realise that their confidence was wearing thin and that within the walls of their immaculate five-star suites, knives were being sharpened. Occasionally she had picked up gossip that had joked about his 'virtual' presence. The schedule had promised a wildlife expedition with an expert naturalist, followed by an 'unforgettable' gourmet experience. She had dealt with the problem by throwing money at it. A small convoy of luxury four-wheel drive cars had been arranged. They were driven to a remote beauty spot in a pine forest overlooking an ethnic village inhabited by Akha hill tribes. At the top of a winding road Amy had arranged to meet up with Cars Van de Velde, a Dutchman who had given up a promising career in shipping to become an ornithologist.

The tall bearded man handed out Swarovski spotting scopes.

"You're in luck", he announced, "We've just come across a rare ribbon-tailed Astrapia."

Originally from New Guinea and similar to a bird-of-paradise, it was unusual to find the species so far north (in fact so unusual it was probably a jailbird from a zoo). They had to hurry, they had to be quiet and they had to refrain from taking pictures; an injunction that piqued the handful of guests that had bothered to lug heavy cameras, tripods and lenses.

After two hot and humid hours traversing a rocky and thorny hillside, they came upon the fabled clearing; a small oasis in the rainforest hidden by long grass and surrounded by pink cassia trees. Akha hunters had got there first. A fire was burning. They were preparing to roast the rare birds, their velvet black plumage already neatly plucked by a group of old women for headdresses and feather dusters. Van de Velde, pushing amongst them, started kicking dirt over the flames. The village headman, with no idea he'd done anything wrong, was anxious to placate the red-faced Dutchman. He offered to sell the birds' tail feathers, snow white and turquoise, unusually long.

Van de Velde stormed into the undergrowth, struggling to find a connection to report the atrocity and have the tribes' people arrested. Amy had to knock some sense into him. Moping over the charred carcasses wasn't going to bring his feathered friends back to life. She did a whip round among her well-heeled guests and procured enough support to fund extra research. It wasn't enough. Van de Velde was looking at a lucrative study grant from the EU going up in flames. Inconsolable, he was last seen trudging up to the main peak, his angry silhouette soon lost in the mists.

Amy led the disgruntled tour group back to the cars, the return journey uphill, hotter and more arduous than before. They got back thirsty, irritable and hungry for the 'gourmet' promise of the day.

A shaded circle in a pine forest had been prepared. Waiters served champagne and gave out specially prepared hampers. To further appease dissent, free wine was offered. The dessert wine, a rare Sauternes, had been especially popular. Loosened up by the alcohol, the party had grown more gregarious and irreverent. Late in the afternoon one of the guests had pretended to dress up as Corran and to the delight of the other guests, had mocked up a gourmet tea using banana leaves and elephant dung. It wasn't a good impersonation. The man had spoken with a French accent. Corran was Australian. But it still grated with Amy. She knew that jokes very quickly soured to resentment and from resentment to calls for a full refund.

Eighteen

Corran returned to the veranda to find his place at the table taken. The young man in his seat had long hair, spider tattoos on his forearms, wore a Def Leopard T-shirt and half-torn jeans. He was introduced as the chef, Timi.

During his call, Dao had obviously over-spun the narrative of Corran's fame. As he approached the table, hands raced for their smart phones. Crowding around Corran, they posed in several set pieces as they swopped around their mobiles. With Dao insisting on squeezing into the already tight frame whichever passing waitresses were at hand, it became a laborious ceremony taking more time than was necessary. Corran had forced a smile, but the conversation with Amy had left him rattled; in the pictures his expression came out looking oddly asymmetrical and pained as if he had just been parboiled in hot water.

The food arrived. Timi organised its placing on the table and reseated himself. Dao, true to his promise, had severely overdone it. The young chef, nervous in Corran's presence and anxious to impress, had supplemented the order with one or two of his own original creations. Dishes, fighting for space, had to be piled up on top of each other, in some places, four to a precarious stack. There was a sweet *yum som-o*, the prawns lightly crisped and sandwiched between delicate segments of pomelo, succulent slices of fresh beef, grilled over a charcoal fire and mixed with thinly cut shallots, coconut, cassia and chilli and two potent soups – a *tom yum kung* and a *kuay tiew*. Already more than enough, this was followed by squid with green mango, duck and tapioca, a fiery chicken and baby corn curry, backed up with several vegetable and tofu dishes.

Despite deriding Dao's very un-Thai-like suggestion to hover over the dishes and randomly pick and choose whatever took his fancy, Corran found himself grabbing his fork and doing exactly that.

The food was good, very good. His taste thresholds might have been damned by a vision of the sublime, but experiencing such giddy heights hadn't totally ruined his ability to appreciate a perfectly acceptable meal.

Unlike Dao, who had family in Chaiyaphum, Timi had come to the area as a stranger. Passing through on his way to Nong Khai then east to Laos and Cambodia, he had never intended to stay for longer than a night. For a favour and running short of cash, he had helped out in a restaurant. The owner, recognising his talent, immediately offered to take him on as a partner. Timi, only midway through his Asian motorbike tour, had politely declined. He'd tried to leave several times. But the owner, desperate to secure his acquiescence, kept hiding his keys. Worn down by these endless tricks, he wearily agreed to consider it. Timi recounted an awkward and embarrassing business meeting at which the owners' two daughters had 'dropped by', ostensibly to use the printer in the office. Both were young, pretty and single. It was left unclear whether they were part of the inducement. Whatever the truth of it, the ruse succeeded. Timi wistfully sold his battered but beloved Honda TransAlp, took over the restaurant and married the youngest daughter. They now had two beautiful children.

Impressed by the dishes, Corran asked where he had got his experience. Timi explained that his parents had sent him to Europe. He had enrolled as a student at a technical college in Bern. Disillusioned with the course (supply chain management and factory inventory), he had dropped out and gravitated towards Paris looking for work. Taking mainly menial tasks in a number of Left Bank restaurants, he had slowly progressed from the basin to the work station, where he started to hone his skills. Corran was surprised to learn that he had worked as one of Pierre Bellisent's team at the Lasserre in Montparnasse. He had visited the restaurant when he was writing an article for an Italian food magazine on the city's rising new talents. Timi was proud that Lasserre's signature dish of Spanish mussels in a green curry sauce was inspired by a meal he had cooked for the chef. Bellissent, grateful for his input, had even credited Timi in the menu.

After four years of building up the business, Timi had acquired some renown in the area. Local dignitaries and famous stars from Bangkok often stopped by to eat at his place. He even had visits from former clients he had known when he worked in Paris. He claimed that Julie Delphy, after filming *Before Midnight*, had taken time off to travel in the Far East. Remembering Timi (in Paris Bellissent had presented the young Thai as the 'architect' of her favourite mussel dish), she had come by for a meal with her family. Corran thought this unlikely. But Timi, casually scrolling through his Instagram account, had the photographs to prove it. Not only had Delphy wrapped her arms around Timi, she looked like she was kissing him on the lips.

Corran checked his watch. It was close to nine. Glancing across at the remaining dishes on the table, he noticed with some relief that the meal was nearing its end. He was tidying up the last plates, soaking up the remaining sauces with a final mouthful of rice, when, to his confusion a second procession of food arrived.

There wasn't enough room. To accommodate the fresh dishes, Timi ordered a move to a larger banqueting table. The shift, moving everyone's drink's and plates, together with the fresh dishes, required a lot of unnecessary work. The restaurant was at its busiest, the waitresses over worked. Corran grabbed a few plates himself to help out. Halfway through making the move they heard the wail of sirens beyond the trees. Flashing blue lights lit up the trees; a motorcade had arrived. Two police motorcycles and a dark grey Mercedes parked up in the small, gravel carpark – Timi's claims that he attracted big-spending clients weren't empty boasts.

As the waitresses began to rearrange the cutlery and place settings, the real reason for the larger table came as an unwelcome shock: the district officer and the police captain now stepping up onto the platform were joining them at the table.

As the two minor dignitaries crossed the veranda, Dao and Timi stood up to greet them. Dao introduced Corran. The 'Very Thai' photo-greeting ceremony was reenacted; again the formal poses were frozen and again the many camera phones exchanged hands. A deputy for the district officer even had a small video camera to record the occasion.

Corran, watching how Dao fawned over these late additions to the meal, was beginning to wake up to his shifty duplicity. The over-ordering hadn't been for his benefit at all. Dao had used the occasion of Corran staying at his hotel to both invite and impress all his important friends and acquaintances. His fame was currency, kudos – maybe that was Thai hospitality?

Chin, the police chief, a severe, gruff-looking man in his late thirties, apologised for being late. The two of them had been guests at the local Muay Thai fight in town. In fact his eight-year-old boy had been in the contest. They had been worried. A lot of expensive bets had been placed. But his son, three kilos overweight for his class, risked being disqualified. Chin's boxing coach had been up all night, pushing the boy through a gruelling sprint up and down the hard shoulder of the motorway in an attempt to shed some extra kilos. Despite running for most of the night, it hadn't worked. Midway through the morning, they had resorted to 'sweating' the distraught boy in a neighbour's corrugated iron pig house. The few kilos saved was still not enough. In the end, it had been simpler to bribe the officials. There had been eight of them; unusual for a small, provincial tournament. But it had been worth it. The boy had won in the fifth round.

Chin, too, had once been a child boxer. He clenched his hands on the table to show off his frighteningly large fists.

They were all hard drinkers. As the evening ground on, beer bottles were replaced by whisky, rum and vodka.

Within the conversations, the subject of Corran's obsessive search came up. Chin was very familiar with the area. In fact the region was close to his mother-in-law's village. Yes, there were lakes. Some of them fed into the town's reservoir. But he was adamant that there were no restaurants.

"Why mess about with such a stupid search?" questioned Chin, spending an inordinate amount of time polishing his precious and seemingly expensive lenses. "Everywhere you look there is good food", he added, waving his arm nonchalantly in the direction of Timi's kitchen. "Right, hah?" he reiterated, nodding at Corran's empty plate.

Corran didn't argue. Ever conscious that he was sitting with Chaiyapum's brightest culinary star, he down played the importance of his quest.

Bao, the district officer, overhearing Chin's words, weighed in. He was more than pleased that someone of Corran's notoriety was interested in the area; he would print a column about the visit in the local government newsletter. Food was good for business. The best places, of course, were in town – Timi's being the only exception. The rest, especially those hidden deep in the countryside, weren't worth bothering about; infested with rats. Besides, it wasn't a good idea for foreigners to sneak about too much. They kept good order in the district. But lately there had been disturbing rumours; gangs from Bangkok were using abandoned houses and rice barns for illegal drug-running – mostly ampethamines, but sometimes crystal meth. After dark, it wasn't safe. For security it was best to stay at the hotel, or to be really safe, a brothel – nothing ever went wrong in the tight embrace of a pretty girl; Isarn was famous for them.

After Bao's lead, the conversation quickly degenerated into guns, girls and golf. Corran, anxious not to come over as too unmanly (their default reading of all Westerners), wasn't totally adverse to racking up the bullish, macho banter. He was also intrigued by the men. As their dialogue became more boastful, Corran sat back in his seat and quietly observed their interaction. Timi, new to the circle, was likely still an outsider. Dao, Chin and Bao clearly had history. They were obviously close and had been for years. Although use of nicknames and comradely back-slapping showed familiarity, small mannerisms and gestures betrayed some hidden tension; a brittle dynamic hinting that beneath the blokey chat and bravado, some terrible misdeed had perhaps thrown them, of necessity, together.

Slowly and imperceptibly, the restaurant took on the appearance of a makeshift nightclub. Tables and chairs were cleared around a small raised rostrum. Coloured disco lights and a glitter ball were switched on. Half an hour later, Dao, Chin and Bao were up on stage, crowding around the single Karaoke microphone, wading through a Thai version of an Abba classic, 'It's a rich man's world'.

Corran was left alone with Timi. After the large meal and drinks they both looked worn and tired. With Dao and his friends now thankfully on stage, relative peace reigned at the table, broken only occasionally by bursts of static from Chin's police walkie-talkie.

Timi used the interlude to return to the conversation Corran had had with Bao about his restaurant search. Some years back, when Timi had first arrived in the area, he thought he might have come by such a place. Corran described what he had seen in more detail; the overgrown approach, the steps up to the veranda, even the half-submerged car in the lake.

"I think I went there," said Timi, "It was when I was still thinking of taking up my father-in-law's offer to take over his place. I drove around the country trying to get a feel for what others were doing."

"How long back?"

"Maybe four years."

"But you didn't return?"

"I think it's gone, closed down. Fallen into ruin."

"Why?"

"It ended badly. I can't remember much. A small piece in the local paper. The usual thing. Some guys got drunk. There was an accident. Maybe that's how the car ended up in the water?"

He reached for his glass again. Corran was silent.

"Then again... A lot of that kind of stuff happens around here. I could have got it wrong."

Nineteen

Corran woke with a jolt, as if someone had passed a high-voltage current through his bedframe. It was oppressively dark. Struggling to make out the four walls of his room, it took him awhile to orientate himself, remember where he was.

He had heard a girl screaming. It was loud, piercing, but as yet he couldn't work out whether it had been in his dreams or had come from outside. Maybe the echo was from the garden? Could the cowboy event still be going on?

Corran rose from the bed. He couldn't find the light switch, so felt his way across the room, stubbing a toe on an open suitcase before reaching the window. Pulling back the curtains, he peered down into the garden. It was empty. In the far corner of the space the stage had been dismantled, the cardboard cut-outs of Buffalo Bill and Pocahontas folded by the pool. Most of the scaffolding had already been dismantled, the steel poles laid to rest in the grass, the speakers and sound equipment stacked in cases ready to be taken out the next day.

Walking back to the bed, Corran sat down on the edge and turned on the overhead spotlights. He thought back to the haunting scream that had disturbed him. Linked to the sound, a face had formed in his memory, but it was faint. He closed his eyes hoping that the dark might help conjure up a coherent form from the shifting shapes in his consciousness. Slowly, like a photographer struggling to fix a picture in a chemical bath, an image coalesced from the murky shadows. He saw water, bubbles rising from the depths, a body slowly sinking, long hair flowing, a face pale, impassive, but not pained, the eyes closed.

The front door of the hotel was locked. No one was around. Corran had to lift himself over the raised marble edge of the reception desk, to reach under the lip of the return to find the entrance keys.

Outside, the air was unusually cold. He found his hire car, started the engine and quietly turned out of the carpark onto the empty high street. With no need for air-conditioning, he wound down the windows.

The chill air, the deserted road and the stillness of the passing scenery veiled in a low hanging haze, gradually dispelled the unease he had felt when he had woken. The release of tension, together with the unorthodox hour, brought an unexpected clarity to his thoughts. Gone was the befuddled indecision of the previous day. Whereas before he had struggled to recall the labyrinth of roads and tracks that had led to the lake restaurant, now the sequence of turns and junctions raced back into his memory with almost cinematic lucidity; the sharp turn off the highway, the billboard with the smiling surfer girl, the peculiar house with the vulgar blue ceramic steps, the shrine folded into the twisted roots of the banyan tree, to the crucial turning where it had all previously gone so painfully wrong – the crossroads marked by the rotten, broken signpost.

But it wasn't just the lay of the land that rushed back with icy vividness. In his mind's eye, he saw Dao, sitting in the seat next to him. He looked different, as if he was seeing his face and expression from an entirely different vantage-point and perspective. No longer the sympathetic profile of a man who had selflessly devoted a busy day to a complete stranger, he now saw nothing but duplicity and guile. Dao had lied about the crossroads. By insisting that the critical turning led to a sugar factory, he had deceived Corran into taking the second junction and not the first. A single error that had led to a catalogue of frustrating mistakes. A day that had culminated in the supposedly 'chance' meeting with Dao's mates at Timi's restaurant. That now looked more suspect. He thought back to the drunken conversations. All those clunky tales of spirits, ghosts and crazed drugs gangs, each with their own narrative designed to unnerve. Were they playing games with him? Did they think him a complete moron that he would fall for such childish deceits? Or was there something else; something more menacing and malign – a veiled warning, threat, that people like himself, foreigners, shouldn't interfere? But interfere with what? Surely his interests, a search for a small, simple restaurant, couldn't be more innocent? Yet they didn't want him to find it. Why?

Having made the correct and crucial turns, Corran's progress from the junction was automatic, without conscious intervention, each remembered feature leading consecutively to the next.

As before, the road climbed through a rubber plantation, passed the rough rag village hidden in the trees, carried over the crest of a hill, before descending into the valley.

It was only at the old wooden bridge over the river that he was forced to slow. Although the waters of the river were now calm, several warning signs (that Corran couldn't read) had been placed to block the passage to the far bank. And almost as if the perpetrator had worried that this might not be enough to deter a determined mind, several rotten planks had been ripped out from the floor of the structure to make it appear more fragile and precarious than it really was. Corran scanned the remaining boards. They looked solid enough. If he kept the car hard to the right he might just make it. But then why risk it?

Corran parked the car and got out. He didn't have his camera pack; not that there was any point – it was highly unlikely that the girl, or anyone else, would still be awake. After all the lies and deception from Dao and his set of 'friends', his only purpose, his single-minded mission, was to prove that he was right and they were wrong; find the location, confirm in his mind that he wasn't going nuts. Remembering that the restaurant wasn't far from the river, he chose to walk.

Locking the hire car, he started across the bridge, one hand gripping the railing, taking care to avoid the gaping holes that had been opened up by the removal of the boards. On both sides, the water, now an ominous jet black, reflected low-hanging trees and higher up, a canopy of stars. A meteorite fell; its glow leaving a smoky blue trail.

Making it to the far side of the bridge, Corran started up the hill. Bright shafts of moonlight, cutting through the leaves, chequered the worn tarmac of the road with soft, abstract patterns. Through the dense undergrowth to his right, a weak glow on the horizon presaged the coming day.

Corran was impressed by the stillness. Tall, majestic palm trees on both sides of the road, no longer menacing silhouettes tossed and tortured by the wind, stood untroubled and serene. Above, small bats and swifts circled through the branches. Further off, high in the boughs of a distant mango tree, he caught sight of red eyes blinking in the black; maybe some kind of monkey.

At the top of the hill, the thick forest thinned out. The road curved around a bend then continued through fields. A collection of low wooden houses was his first clear indicator that he was getting close. And just beyond, he recognised the clearing where he had first parked his car; the recent indentations in the sand perhaps his own tyre marks.

A calming breeze, the scent of wild jasmine entwined around bushes and the ever-present rattle of cicadas, all confirmed to his senses that he was back in the right place.

Corran stepped off the road and took the track through the long grass. Dense vegetation, shadowing the path from the moonlight, made it difficult to see. He took out his mobile and illuminated the screen, but its faint glow made little or no difference. Up to that point, his train of thought, so certain, so assured, wavered. He slowed. The ground beneath his feet felt somehow different, rougher and strangely uneven. And he'd gone a long way in. The steps to the veranda should have been to his right. Had he strayed too far?

Corran, sensing he'd made a wrong turn, stalled. Suddenly there was movement directly ahead. Something, or someone, was crouched up in the thick grass watching him; something large, something hostile. Warnings from the night before, of spirits, forest demons and Chinese drug gangs, fuelled his imagination. Disturbed by these fears, his mind raced to make sense of the shadow. Whatever it was, shifted slightly to one side. Momentarily silhouetted against a bush, he thought he saw fur – a wild dog, a big cat, even a bear? Rattled that it might be some predator (his knowledge of Thai mammals was vague), Corran retreated a step.

For seconds there was silence. Nothing happened. Taking time to compose himself, he caught his breath and calmed. The brief lull gave Corran time to rationalise his thoughts. There was a breeze blowing. Moonlight flickering through the trees was probably playing tricks with his sight. Psyched-up by anxieties, he had over-reacted. The shape, or thing, was probably nothing more than the shadow of a twisted tree stump or rock. The incident with the hire car in the storm came to mind; hadn't he stupidly mistaken a falling palm branch for a child?

Emboldened by this logic, Corran edged forward, stamping his feet and shaking the bushes. A deep, guttural growl quickly shattered his wishful thinking. The long grass parted. The sinister black shape leapt from the ground.

Corran had been mauled by an animal before. He was six years old. It had happened at his family's home on the edge of Campbelltown south of Sydney. The 'beast' was his stepmother's much-loved Jack Russell. It was a weekend – a Sunday. As a small luxury, his parents liked to have breakfast in bed. His father did the cooking (the only cooking he could do) – fried eggs, fried toast, fried sausages, fried potatoes and thick, streaky, fatty bacon. His stepmother, ever watchful of her hour-glass figure, never ate the toast and always cut the rind off her bacon, mana from heaven for the under-fed canine. This event evolved into a weekly ritual. At nine o'clock sharp, the hungry Jack Russell would station itself on the landing outside the bedroom door in anticipation of this special weekend treat. Corran, bored in his room and up since dawn, knew this. When the promised plate emerged from the corner of the door, he got there first, cruelly blocking the plate from the salivating dog. Like angry wolves, they had fought over the leftovers. Mischievously, Corran taunted the small animal by dangling a slice of bacon from the side of his mouth. The dog, literally driven out of its small demented brain by the boy's maddening horseplay, made a last, desperate bite for the rind. Inadvertently, his jaws closed across the side of Corran's face. The resultant wound explained the lifelong scar Corran possessed across his right cheek.

More than anything, Corran remembered the surgery. The small, prefabricated clinic was close to his school on the edge of town. Being Sunday they were forced to wait three hours for the doctor to do the stitches. There were few comics in the waiting room; most were worn, well-thumbed pony magazines for adolescent girls. The acrid smell of antiseptic and idoform disinfectant immediately made him feel sick; ever since he had developed a deep aversion for hospitals.

Of course, Corran tried to make it up with the dog. But the Jack Russell, the trauma indelibly incised in its primitive, binary brain, never forgave the transgression. Nor were they friends again. The pet's sense of betrayal and distrust was complete and irredeemable. Even in its most desperate state of hunger, when his father and stepmother went away for long weekends in their restored VW campervan, the small hound refused to accept bacon, or, indeed any food, from Corran; it would rather suffer and starve.

Corran came to in the back of a police pick-up. The sun had just risen. A blue light flashed intermittently on the surrounding bushes. Feeling a throbbing pain, he reached to his forehead. He was bleeding from a cut above his eye. A crude bandage had been applied to staunch the flow of blood. The driver, hearing Corran sit up, glanced back over his shoulder. Corran's recognised Chin's deputy.

"You lucky, very lucky," he grunted. "Something attack you. We scare it off."

There was a tap at the glass. Corran turned and saw Chin, looking smug, puffed up, grinning like an over-fed cat. The police captain opened the door of the cab, took off his hat and slid onto the seat next to him.

"Something to show you," he muttered.

Chin reached for his mobile and opened the camera app. Leaning close to Corran, he scrolled through several pictures. They showed the interior of the kitchen by the lake. Plastic bags and cardboard boxes were spread out over the table surface. A close-up showed several heavy bags filled with thousands of pastel-coloured pills.

"We been watching this place a long time. We were lucky. Caught them just as they were moving out. Maybe they had a tip-off. We still caught two of them."

His last picture showed a handcuffed girl – thin, long-haired, fierce, being led to a police car.

"She the one?", asked Chin tapping the screen to focus on her face.

"No," replied Corran.

Chin put his mobile away and reached for the door handle. Peering over the top of his sunglasses, he glanced back at Corran.

"I thought we told you..."

"What?"

"To never come back here."

Twenty

News of the incident got out early. Dao, who had already had a call from Chin, organised a doctor from the local hospital to check Corran's grazes and cuts for infection. The medic had wanted to give a rabies and tetanus shot, but when they had worked out that the dramatic bleeding across his forehead was caused by the fall rather than a vicious bite, he had prescribed the usual cocktail of painkillers, antibiotics and vitamin pills.

Timi, passing through the hotel with early morning deliveries, had joined Corran for breakfast.

"It must have been a big dog. Or a wild pig? There are wild pigs from the hills," suggested Timi reaching for a donut.

"It jumped."

"A bear?"

"Do bears jump?"

The last time Timi had seen such an animal was a small Laotian sun bear dancing on a chain in the weekend market. 'Dancing' might not be the word; the bear, intentionally starved, was struggling to lick honey from a spoon stuck on a bamboo stick, cruelly suspended just out of reach by a small giggling girl.

Corran's big scare had taken up most of the conversation. And judging by the anxious and over-sympathetic looks from passing waitresses and staff, Dao had obviously told everyone; probably typed it up in bold on the morning agenda at the staff meeting. To escape the fawning attention, Corran wanted to get out of the place. He mentioned the possibility of visiting the food market. Timi, going there anyway, offered to take him.

Corran had several reasons for going to the market. The first was practical. Suspecting that it was Chin's thugs who had dressed up the lakeside location as some kind of crack den, it was highly unlikely the girl would be returning to the place any time soon. That now made it impossible to glean any knowledge from a return to the kitchen. He would have to probe deeper. Her ingredients must have come from somewhere. There was a good chance that some of them had come from the town. Timi agreed. A frequent visitor to the market, he had several contacts who specialised in rare spices, roots and wild herbs.

The second reason was a hunch, a long shot, that Corran kept to himself. When he had sneaked into the kitchen shack at the lakeside restaurant two nights ago, he remembered seeing a well-used motorcycle helmet on a shelf by the door. If the girl had a crash helmet, she must have owned a small scooter. A 50cc bike would have given her a mobility that would most likely have been local. And if he'd taken a set of dividers and made a circumference around the area of the lake and the comfortable range of such a modest machine laden with shopping bags, she wouldn't go far; Chaiyaphum would have been her market of choice. She might be there.

Twenty One

The two large warehouses of Chaiyaphum's market were situated on the outskirts of town. By the time Timi and Corran had driven there and squeezed into a last remaining space, it was already sweltering under the heat of the midday sun.

The market stalls, running in long thin lines, were densely packed into a regimented grid of raw concrete aisles. Above the stalls, thin mesh frames held up a patchwork roof of faded canvas and half-torn PVC. Winding their way across the different aisles, a confused mesh of electrical cables, junction boxes and plugs powered the lights of the stalls. Sticky and humid, the concrete floors were damp with scuffed cardboard and rotten vegetable waste.

They'd set off too late. Corran wasn't prepared for the crowds. Lunchtime workers were already filling the food aisles. Steam and spitting oil hissed from huge woks dotted across the stalls. Butterfly chicken, crispy pork, cuts of beef and salted fish, shared space with deep-fried crabs, worms, lizards and small birds.

You were out of luck if you were reincarnated as one of god's creatures in Thailand. Whatever you were reborn as – mammal, primate, predator, winged creature, finned creature, bugs with many legs, grubs with no legs – and whether you lived out the creator's allotted time in fields, lakes, bushes or tree stumps, it was more than likely that you would end your days getting crisp and brown in a deep-fat frying pan in some little known town like Chaiyaphum.

Timi led the way through the alleyways. Corran, following and ever inquisitive, scanned the stalls and tables as they passed. Peering over peoples' shoulders, he checked out what they were eating – the curries and soups, the different styles of noodle, and the sauces and spices (*nam chim*) that accompanied them.

The turnover was fast; junior office workers, minor officials and off-duty police officers shared tables with teachers and students. People ate quickly, there was little conversation and, due to the heat and humidity, no one stayed long.

Corran, looking through the crowds, thought he caught sight of Dao, Chin and Bao. Huddled together at a noodle stand, they appeared deep in conversation. Bao had even looked up and he was sure for a split second the man had recognised him; Corran, as the only pale face in the place, wouldn't have been hard to catch sight of. Turning the corner of the aisle, Corran had intended to shout out to them, to try and find his way round to their table, but by the time he had looked back they had gone. He didn't look further; Timi, already some way ahead, was fast leaving him behind. Quickening his pace, he rushed to catch up.

The food stalls gave way to the general market. Printed T-shirts, dresses and jeans mixed with cheap fashion accessories and glitzy jewellery. Drawn deeper into the maze, they passed stalls selling dolls, robots and toy cars. A further section had tables laid out with secondhand comics, old fashion magazines and books. He even chanced upon an edition of his own book, *Good in Sixty Seconds*. Wrapped in thin cellophane and with a sticker price handwritten in Thai, the cover looked worn and well thumbed. It was a salutary lesson. He never imagined his works would have arrived at this sad fate – unloved, half-price and gathering dust on a forgotten street stall.

Seeing his book in the market triggered deeper anxieties; his tortured and yet unfinished manuscript that should have been sent to New York, the antagonism with the Lescari crowd and, of course, Amy.

Corran remembered with a certain dread the promises he'd made, how he'd given his word that he would meet her in Nong Khai in the evening. The town was over four hundred kilometres away. To make it he should have left hours ago. What the hell was he still doing there? Instinctively, he reached into his pocket for his mobile. The usual lines of missed calls filled the screen. His thumb hovered over the call-back icon, but glancing ahead he saw that he was yet again losing sight of his guide. It would have to wait. Slipping the iPhone back into his pocket, he sprinted to close the gap.

Eventually, an unlikely passage at the end of the pets' section (stacked cages of sad fluffy things: English Spaniels, Pugs and Labradoodles panting in the tropical heat), led through a labyrinth of thin corridors to a second, smaller warehouse behind. After the teeming intensity of the main market, the open spaces of the spice hall came as a welcome relief. With tall, corrugated roofs, the place offered both air, shade and sanity. And with the lunch-time food stalls now some distance away, the interior was both quieter and less frenetic.

Corran was no stranger to Asian spices and herbs. For one of his earliest programmes he had travelled the southern spice route from Kerala, across the Indian Ocean and the Persian Gulf, then overland to the Mediterranean and Venice. The trade in cinnamon, cassia, ginger, black pepper and turmeric, the equivalent of the modern-day movement of microchips, silicon and lithium, had created private fortunes, palaces and imperial cities along its way.

Jacob Fugger, citizen of modest Augsburg, became one of the richest men in the world, if not the richest man of all time (beating today's Zuckerberg's and Abramovich's by relative wealth), in relocating this lucrative market from Venice to Lisbon in the 15th century. Of equal significance to the future of cuisine, was the movement not just of the ingredients, but the seeds and plants themselves across the continents. When the wily Portuguese adventurer, Vasco de Gama, had the temerity to ask the Zamorin of Calicut for a pepper plant, his followers, anxious to protect their crucial monopoly, were horrified. Yet the ruler, knowing that Kerala's unique conditions (unearthly downpours from twin monsoons) were essential for the plants success, remained unruffled, "You can take our pepper, but you will never be able to take our rains."

History would prove the proud Zamorin wrong: today the trade in black pepper (Black gold as it was then known) is dominated by Vietnam – famous for its thunderous and torrential floods.

Other well-known spices have also been shamelessly appropriated by other nations: ginger, indigenous to China, is part of West African and Caribbean cuisine, Japanese tempura was borrowed from Portugal, and chillies, originally from South America, have been celebrated and claimed as part of Thailand's cultural and national heritage.

Although the spice market of small town Chaiyaphum didn't register on anyone's cultural radar, Corran was still taken aback by its scale. Even before he had had a chance to explore the rarer ingredients – the roots, funguses, tree leaves and nuts – he was dazzled enough by the variety and colour of just the well-known basics. Large trays of dried peppercorns, from the sumak lemon pepper to the richer *phrik thai on*, covered at least five stalls. And then there were his favourites, tall, radiant pyramids of piled-up chillis. From the deep red, and intensely potent, *phrik khi nu*, to the larger pale green wax pepper, *phrik yuak* and the orange-yellow, *prik leuang*, woven bamboo trays displayed practically every size, shape and colour variation in between.

Pulled between different aisles and stalls, where larger, even more lavish arrangements caught his eye, Corran took his time, bending low over the different trays to absorb the distinct aromas.

For celebrity chefs, those who had built international reputations and lucrative careers off Thai cuisine, the chemistry of spices, sauces and herbs sat at the heart of their art. Whether recipes were designed to impart sweetness, sourness, spiciness, bitterness or saltiness, it was the fusion of such tastes and the craft with which they were processed and refined that contributed to the balance, depth and resonance of the final dish. Thai cooking, taken to extremes, was like Thai art – time-consuming, meticulous, often fussy, but ultimately intense and melodramatic.

Timi knew most of the stallholders. Aware that the sight of a foreigner sniffing and prodding their produce might create a bit of a stir, he let Corran wander. Women shouted out; who was this handsome stranger, the blonde-haired one who looked like Leonardo DiCaprio? Timi told them he was from Australia, that he was a world-famous chef and had at least two million likes on Facebook. The fame didn't impress. But the Facebook likes stirred up a wave of shrieks, whistles and good-natured cackling. The more adventurous tugged at his arms and cried out for photos. Timi, impatient to keep going, had to turn back to rescue Corran from the swarm of attention.

They headed for a discreet corner of the warehouse. The stall they entered was unusual in that it was enclosed, was lockable and mercifully for Corran, had arctic grade air-conditioning. Old Chinese cabinets, set with hundreds of drawers, lined the modest wall space. It was run by a small, wizened old woman dressed as if in mourning. A young girl was with her, possibly her grandchild. Exercise books, illustrated with coloured penguins, hippos and crocodiles, were spread out over the tiled floor. Lying on her front, the girl was finishing her maths homework.

The old woman greeted Timi warmly, but was more circumspect when she saw Corran. She quickly surmised that the 'foreigner' must have been the cause of the trouble outside. She didn't know many *farang*, and those she did made her feel unwell. To put her mind at ease, Timi sketched out his background, though downplayed the fame. Without dwelling on the details, he touched on Corran's experience at the lakeside restaurant, which had led to his interest in Thai herbs and spices. Looking him up and down she asked why someone from a big international city might be interested in an insignificant cafe. Timi replied that it was for a book he was writing, *The Story of Food*, with recipes from more than three hundred countries.

The woman was bemused by his inflated ambitions; foreigners were like that – from simple sugared drinks to cupcakes – they weren't happy selling to a small group of friends, they had to trade with every one, with the billions. Her circle was all in her head. She knew everyone of her customers. She was happy with that scale. One day she would write a book – one book with one recipe on one page, just for her granddaughter. And it was going to be way better than his.

A kettle was boiled and tea served. As the three sipped from small china cups, Timi and the old woman gossiped. They talked about family, scandals, marriages and deaths, before moving onto more serious topics – her numerous and complex medical conditions. Timi, sensing that she was still wary of Corran, slowly steered the conversation back to her impressive collection of herbs and spices.

When she had first set up her stall forty years ago, it was never her intention to become anything like a well-known 'specialist'. The very idea made her squirm; you either knew your stuff or you didn't. Collecting things purely out of curiosity, she was constantly surprised that people would travel hundreds of miles merely to seek her advice. With contacts among a handful of Chinese, Burmese and Indian merchants, her knowledge and reach had extended. A map pinned to a board and crudely coloured with crayons (probably by her daughter), displayed the extent of her 'empire'. And that 'empire' was wrapped up in the small drawers of her cabinet. At intervals she broke from the conversation, reached for a distant drawer, opened it, sniffed the contents, then placed a sachet on the table for Timi to sample. From the familiar, bitter Vietnamese *rau chin* and elephant ear stalks; to the rarer, cassia cinnamon, balsam seeds and Japanese wasabia; the selection moved to the weird – red ants' eggs, dried fish eyes and bee larvae.

Engrossed in their conversation, they acted as if Corran didn't exist. Left alone he tried helping out with the girl's homework, but her level of maths (she was nine), was already past his limited ability. Giving up on the algebra, his attention drifted over the walls of the cramped space. Scanning the shelves and cupboards, he noticed that one particular cabinet at the back of the room was left untouched. With lacquered teak as black as night, its doors were inlaid with mother of pearl, the silver slithers tracing the outlines of snakes and tigers. A large padlock over its doors intrigued him most. He lent closer to Timi, wanting to know what was inside. Timi discouraged him; not only was it illegal, it would also disgust him (the nacre inlays should have provided a clue).

Corran's unsolicited intrusion reminded the old woman of the foreigner's irksome presence. She'd done enough talking anyway. Sinking back into her padded swivel chair, she returned to her tea.

"How much do you want?" she asked Timi.

Timi replied that it wasn't for him it was for Corran.

"How much does he want?" she corrected.

"All of it," replied Corran.

The woman grunted disapprovingly, she didn't like brashness. Glancing critically in his direction, her suspicions returned; why did he want so much, where was he taking it, what was he going to do with it, how would she replenish her precious stocks?

Catching sight of a line of crisp 1,000 baht bills on the cold marble table top changed her tune; though such abject surrender wasn't immediate. It took a second line of fresh notes before a grudging, almost imperceptible nod showed that the offer was accepted. Turning to her granddaughter, she insisted on having the money recounted. The young girl, scooping up the neat piles, was enthralled by the pristine notes; she'd never seen so much money. Methodically arranging the bills into houses of ten she gleefully confirmed the amount. For her diligence, Corran sneaked her an additional five hundred. She ran off to buy sticky sweets, despite her grandmother's obvious disapproval.

Twenty Two

The aluminium door slid open. Corran and Timi stepped out of the interior, the fierce heat of the main spice market invading grandma's icy refuge.

Timi needed to do a number of his own errands. He offered to share Corran's bags and help guide him back to the main exit to catch a taxi. Corran, confident he could make it out alone, assured him he would be okay. Timi wished him good luck and left.

Lifting his bags for the first time, Corran was shocked to discover their true weight. They might only have contained light sachets, but the old woman had wrapped everything in layers of heavy and unnecessary packaging, sometimes wooden boxes. He looked across the building and caught sight of the chef in the far distance, too far to call back. The rejection of Timi's second offer, to guide him out of the maze, was his second regret. By the time he'd even struggled to the end of the hall, he was already floundering. And his first turn only exacerbated his problems.

The error led Corran to the back of the meat market. The avenues of stalls, teeming with sellers, butchers and porters, were noisy, cluttered and claustrophobic. Rows of fleshy carcasses hung limp from metal hooks. In a second corridor, lines of glazed ducks and chickens were crushed together like rush-hour commuters. A steel table top displayed a batch of fresh pigs' snouts; the thick skin from their noses peeled away like rubber from their pulpy, pallid faces. Just behind this gruesome arrangement, a tin tray of pink trotters lay neatly bound with delicate red bows. Corran, choosing not to dwell too long on some of the more obscure body parts dangling just inches above, searched for an exit.

Passing a butcher's block, Corran caught a blood-curdling squeal. Out of the corner of his eye he saw a meat cleaver fall. He heard the dull thud of the blade hitting the wood board and the crunch of severed vertebra. He didn't see the dead animal, but he felt a fine spray of warm blood softly coating his forearm. Did a slither of bone lodge in his hair near his ear?

Feeling the sweat on his forehead, he became aware of how hot he was. More than the heat was the stress. Everywhere he looked, macabre sights assailed him – flies and mosquitoes everywhere, pale fleshy cuts in sickly boiling broths, coagulated blood seeping into the walkways.

Overwhelmed by the stench of the place, he was beginning to feel nauseous. His head was spinning, he heard a piercing ringing between his ears. Searching the stalls he looked for a seat. He found a plastic stool and slumped down. His head fell to his hands.

Minutes passed. Eventually raised voices made Corran look up. A sea of concerned faces surrounded him. Everyone was talking and gesturing in different directions. A woman held out a glass of water. Next to her an old man pushed forward a battered first-aid tin with plasters, ointment and a collection of unfamiliar pills. Another offered a packet of coloured throat pastilles. Still dazed Corran struggled to sit upright. The water was closest. Refreshingly cool, it was surprisingly effective. He was obviously dehydrated. The woman, seeing the change come over him, began splashing his forehead directly from the bottle. She went too far. He had to hold his hands up to discourage her. The liquid stung his eyes, it obviously wasn't water.

As the ringing in his head calmed, he was able to stand. The circle around him, the woman and the old man with the first aid box, began to drift away. A fresh breeze blew through the musky aisles. Clearing the air, the wind grew strong enough to lift the edge of a tarpaulin on the side of the warehouse. The gap in the blinds opened up a view to the countryside, a comforting vista of swaying coconut palms, blue sky and clouds.

Taking deep breaths and assured that deliverance was near, his strength and confidence returned. Of course, what had disgusted him was still there on all sides, but having suffered and survived a near-fainting fit, he was somehow more immune to its horrors.

With his anxieties reined in, more sensible thoughts coalesced. He began to make plans again. Released from the horror of the meat hall, it wouldn't take long to get back to the hotel. In less than twenty minutes he could pack, pay the bill and be back on the road. If he drove hard, he might stand a chance of making the evening rendezvous with Amy and the tour group, perhaps even restore some of his tarnished credibility. Then he'd call Callister in New York, grovel a bit, show some contrition, mend the broken bridges. Ok, he hadn't managed to get back to the lakeside restaurant and the girl, but his venture hadn't been a total catastrophe. Within the sachets of rare herbs and spices he had bought from the recalcitrant grandmother, he was bound to unearth some of her secrets.

He was racing to the exit, when a last distraction caught his eye. A stall was selling the local speciality, the famous spicy sausage, the *sai krok priao* and *sai krok isarn*. Stacked up in neat circular coils, they looked like so many sleeping serpents. He wanted to buy one, but with so little time (there were already several shoppers obediently queuing in front of him), resorted to a quick photo. Reaching for his phone he stepped closer. He was framing up the shot at the front of the display (the backlight needed some adjustment), when suddenly, surreally framed at the centre of a heart-shaped window of fermented pork sausage, he saw a face, previously in shadow, that caught the sun. In truth, it was less than a face, it was a glimpse of hair lifted by the breeze, the corner of a mouth, the glow from a golden iris – the girl from the restaurant. Seeing her made him jump back, an involuntary reflex that had him hitting the back of his head against the top of the sausage stall. The bamboo uprights shook violently, knocking precious products onto the floor. The shop owner, breaking from a customer, screamed, "AAAeiiiiii! AAeiiii!". Corran turned to apologise. By the time he looked back, she had gone.

Dropping everything, he ran. If he moved fast he could easily catch her. She was just walking – and slowly. In such a short space of time she couldn't possibly get far. His biggest problem was the layout of the market, he was on the wrong side of the aisle. If he was going to reach her, he would have to run down the length of the stalls and double back on himself.

He made good headway on the first straight – it was clear and mercifully dry. But on sprinting around the corner of the aisle, he found the avenue blocked. A porter, taking a break from his deliveries, had parked a trolley of stacked fish near a stall. There was a thin gap to the left of the trolley if he was quick. He accelerated.

The fish porter, hearing the thump of approaching footsteps, turned. Shocked by the sight of such a large white man thundering towards him, he panicked and pushed the cart away from him. Corran, seeing the gap close, tried to stop, but the floor, layered with an effervescent mix of putrefying waste and grease, was as slippery as a skating rink. Unable to arrest his speed, he rammed hard into the side of the trolley. The trays of stinky, salty mackerel unbalanced and fell over his face and chest.

Corran brushed off the festering fish and staggered to his feet. The fish porter was screaming at him. Not understanding a word the man was saying, Corran muttered an apology and ran on. Reaching the end of the aisle, a bottle of soy flew past his shoulder missing him by inches. A second was better aimed, grazing the side of his head, before shattering on a concrete post. Black sauce sprayed over his white T-shirt. A drop hit his lower lip, tasting sharp and bitter like squid ink, unusually astringent.

Corran made it around the corner and doubled back. But the delay had been damaging. By the time he had got back to the place where he had last seen the girl's haunting profile, she was nowhere to be seen. Spinning around, his eyes searched all the possible paths and exits she could have used. To his right, a group of people were queuing for lottery tickets. He ran over and searched the line – she wasn't there. Running back, he checked the adjacent aisle. Five minutes at least had passed. Maybe she had already made for the exit and was no longer in the building? An opening in the distance suggested that possibility. Hanging from a gantry, a neon arrow highlighted the gateway to the car park.

Again the geography of the aisles, with their rigidly aligned rows, didn't make it easy. He could see the exit – it wasn't far. But to get there quickly meant heading back the way he had come. If he could get over the row in front of him it would be a shortcut, gaining valuable time. Corran grabbed the upright of a market stall in an attempt to swing himself over the counter. It was the kind of effortless manoeuvre he had seen performed on TV the world over. But the wooden post, too fragile to take his weight, splintered and came away in his hand. Slipping back, his sudden weight on the side of the table unbalanced the stand. Bamboo cages sitting on its shelves came loose and fell to the floor. Delicate doors, secured with thin wooden wedges, snapped open. As he rolled across the concrete he saw lizards – bright green ones with yellow frills – racing quickly for the shadows. A thinner streak of vivid green was possibly a snake, he hoped not venomous.

Picking himself up from the sticky surface, the angry reptile seller took a swing at him. He was reaching for a bigger club when Corran slipped past, vainly holding up his arms in atonement.

Seconds later, Corran made it to the entrance gate and emerged into the sunlight. Against all the odds, his plan had worked. By bypassing the long central aisle he was on the threshold of the exit. More incredibly still, he saw the girl again. She was heading towards the bus stop on the far side of the open ground.

Corran sprinted into the car park. As he weaved through the dense throng of scooters, *tuk tuk's* and taxis, a piercing horn howled behind. Jumping to the side, a truck, stacked high with cassava roots, lumbered by, its trailer missing him by inches. Turning, he darted around the back of the dusty ten-wheeler and emerged on the far side of the road. Pushing though a mass of shoppers, he caught sight of her again. The girl, now just yards in front, stood in a crowd of people waiting at the steps of a bus. Corran, crossing the last divide between himself and the queue of shoppers, reached the top of the line just as she was about to board the coach. As her foot touched the first rung of the steps, he grabbed her arm. Naturally she screamed, a long, piercing shriek that froze the bystanders on both sides. A small face twisted around, its features wrinkled, tired, snarling and fierce – the face of an old woman.

The truth didn't sink in immediately. Corran was so stunned by the woman's miserable, even hideous appearance, and her unnerving howling, that it took him a while to release his grip. The crowd, shaken by his behaviour, had to prise them apart. Not wanting to touch the sweaty foreigner with their hands, they used their packages and bags to lever them apart. The old woman, pulling away, scuttled to the back of the coach and covering her face with a scarf, dived behind the seats.

Corran, baffled and frustrated, retreated. The queue of people quickly flowed around him. The driver, closing the doors and calming his traumatised passengers, started the engine and hit the accelerator. A cloud of sooty diesel exhaust kicked out from the back of the bus. Corran could feel the sticky fumes enveloping him. Glowering faces looked down from the windows as the coach rumbled off.

Corran stepped back. How did that happen? How could he have made such a mistake? He was so close. He was sure it was her. Did she realise he was chasing her? Had she played some kind of game, tricking him by swapping places at the last minute?

From the direction of the marketplace, loud, angry voices converged; the butcher, the reptile-seller and the fish porter were all heading in his direction. Their shouts had attracted the attention of a traffic officer. Leaving his station at the roundabout, he was walking down the concrete ramp to the car park, right hand reaching for his walkie-talkie.

Twenty Three

Dao went to pick up Corran from the Muang Chaiyaphum police station late in the afternoon. He asked for Chin, but was told he was away; the man had important business to attend to in another province. His deputy stood in to help them out. Although the incident at the marketplace was considered a minor transgression, there were several forms to be filled in, pictures to be taken and fingerprints made. Dao started off by translating the complex paperwork together with the statements from the stall-holders, but it proved too tedious for everyone, plaintiffs and police alike. All had better things to do. So Dao ended up signing most of the pages in Corran's name. The concluding stage of the complaints procedure involved handing out several envelopes of cash (Corran's 1,000 baht bills again came in handy). Only then did the disgruntled stallholders break a smile – it was more money than they'd normally make in a month. The charges against Corran were quietly dropped – they were pleased enough to shake hands. Several went straight to a bar.

Corran came back through the doors of the Namsai Hotel shuffling his feet and looking morose. He didn't expect to see Amy. Somehow she'd found him; she was the last person in the world that he wanted to see.

Leaning against the reception desk, she was on her mobile and turned when he walked in. Even from a distance he could sense her rebuke – a great wave of negativity pulsed from her frame like heat from a radiator. Her hair, newly cut, was so perfectly symmetrical that it looked like one of the cheap synthetic wigs he had seen in the market for less than forty baht. An expensive suit and impressive heels added to an air of cold severity. Apart from her clothes, she looked a better version of herself – poise, shape, profile, a holistic upgrade accentuated by his own slovenly stance.

Putting away her mobile, Amy's eyes widened as she took in Corran's shabby appearance. He looked chaotic. His hair was dishevelled, his face smeared with dirt and his previously pristine white t-shirt, scuffed by the oily mackerel fillets, gave off a disturbingly pungent odour. Specks of pig's blood running down his forearm made it look as if he had been in a fist fight.

Disconcertingly Amy didn't say anything. She looked him up and down and walked away.

Midway across the foyer, he caught up.

"I can explain everything," was all he could blandly say.

They sat at a table in the garden, shaded from the heat of the overhead sun by tall, fluted fan palms. Corran, sure in his mind that he had never directly revealed the name of the hotel, was still struggling to work out how Amy had found him. She calmly pointed out that she had caught the name of the town from the tail end of one of his erratic calls. Quickly realising that his situation was spinning out of control, she had been forced to abandon her luxury paying guests at the Nong Khai resort, changing the schedule at the last minute to give them a 'day at their own leisure'. By then, two couples, having given up hope that their 'fantasy' chef would ever show up, had already abandoned the group. Dutifully she had got up early to wave them off and help with their bags, but they had secretly left in the night, leaving a post-it note on her door that they intended to sue.

Borrowing a car from the hotel, Amy had driven south. It had taken her more than six hours. Finding his hotel hadn't been easy. She had spent most of the day driving up and down the high street, parking up in front of likely-looking locations and methodically checking through foreign names in reception-desk registers. She had almost given up hope when, coming out of the Namsai, she was lucky to meet Dao on his way out to collect Corran from the police station. He had offered to take her too. But because she had a backlog of important emails to attend to, she thought it better to wait at the hotel for his return.

Her simple narrative stopped there. She sat back in her seat, finished her tea and, with a look of icy detachment, munched some dark chocolate florentines – on the road at midday she'd missed lunch.

Corran shifted uneasily. Like a boxer tensed for a surprise punch, he felt somewhat relieved. Expecting a storm of rebuke for his errant behaviour, he had been stacking up excuses powerpoint style as she spok – yes, he was guilty; yes, he had been unthinking and negligent; yes, of course he should apologise – but (and he paused here for effect) at the end of the day, what was true professionalism? Surely the integrity of the words and pictures on the page, the best possible result – wasn't that the ultimate goal?

Amy heard him out. She didn't interrupt. When he concluded she didn't fight back, argue, even answer. She just smiled. Why would she smile? It disconcerted him.

They were interrupted. While they had been in conversation, Dao had been able to get through to his friend, the police captain. Chin had cut short his important meeting in Khon Kaen and was already on his way back. Knowing that the issue of the restaurant was, for some reason, still causing Corran some "unhappiness", he had broken with official procedure to allow him and Amy to visit the site. He would meet them there. Hopefully seeing the place and the evidence left by the drug gang *in situ* would put Corran's mind at ease, bring an end to his uncertainty and allow them both to leave Chaiyaphum and continue onto their undoubtedly more important work in Nong Khai.

"Closure," wasn't that what Westerner's wanted?

Twenty Four

A single policeman, fresh out of graduate training, was the only official on duty when Chin's black Mercedes and Corran's Toyota rolled onto the worn grass verge in the late afternoon. Not expecting visitors at the end of the day and unclear as to how long he should stay guarding the site, the cadet had sprawled himself across the front seats of his squad car to watch YouTube on his smartphone. Seeing the distinctive badge of Chin's car so close in the wing mirror startled him. Racing to do up the buttons on his jacket, he grabbed his cap, left the car and ran down the track to lift the cordon of bright yellow tape that had been tied around trees leading up to the lakeside veranda.

Dao and Chin, taking their time to get out of the Mercedes, looked on impassively as Corran led Amy down the rough, overgrown path. Corran, troubled by Chin's claims, was first up the steps. At the top of the platform he looked over the lake. Deprived of its aura of eerie mystery by the harsh overhead sun, the location looked dull, somewhat ordinary. Whereas previously the inky darkness of the lake had reflected a romantic moon and a clear night filled with stars, now there was nothing but a grim, disconsolate, muddy expanse, punctuated with refuse. The protruding bonnet of the car was still there. But daylight also betrayed oil drums, an old computer screen, a fridge door. The pink water lilies that had previously appeared so captivating, were in reality the sole survivors of an abundance of plants that were now mostly shrivelled and dead. The far side of the lake looked even more neglected. The sandbank had fallen away. Deep tyre marks showed where a pick-up had backed up and emptied a truck load of building rubble into the swampy shallows.

On the veranda itself there were still tables and chairs. But they were far fewer than he had remembered, the pieces scattered randomly across the rotten floorboards without any order or purpose.

Amy joined Corran by the railings. Never expecting a designer paradise, she was still stunned by the state of the place. And then there was the smell – a noxious scent of listless, fetid waters mixing with the mouldy stench of decay from the cracked plant pots.

"This place doesn't look like it's been used for years..." she reflected.

"It was here, Amy. I tell you, it was here," whispered Corran glancing warily over his shoulder.

Dao and Chin, shuffling slowly up the steps, joined them on the veranda. Taking seats at a table in the shade, they kept their distance. Chin lit a cigarette. Between puffs, he glanced over, his smug "didn't I tell you dumb foreigner" expression now permanently baked across his craggy face.

Corran, sensing their contemptuous looks, crossed the walkway and headed for the kitchen block. Although he knew Chin's men would likely have crawled all over the place, he still hoped to find some evidence that would link it to that critical night, now two days ago.

He pushed open the main door and walked in, his eyes taking time to adjust to the low light. Although he could clearly see that it was the same room he had been in before, it was far from how he remembered it. The modest wash basin, the charcoal stove and the chopping board had all gone. Beer cans, empty whisky bottles and cigarette stubs littered the floor. At the centre of the shack, a large blue, plastic barrel, a stack of tetra boxes, packing materials and some battered weighing scales supported the police claims that it had been used as a drugs den, as did a small gas hob, pans and mixing flasks filling a side table.

On the walls of the room, pin-up photos of glamour girls from magazines had been taped to the wood. Corran stepped closer to the images. They were yellowed and faded. Chin's men must have stuck them there. He reached up and tore one of the pictures away from the wall. It left a prominent 'shadow' mark on the surface – clear evidence, if it were needed, that they had been up there for years. How could Corran have missed it?

Chin and Dao sidled into the small space, followed by Amy. Chin, finishing a text message, put away his mobile. Quietly he took Corran aside, his eyes doleful, as if genuinely concerned and wanting to be supportive.

"I've just had a message from head office," he whispered. "They finished interviewing the gang members. They confessed. The main boss guy said they had been using this place a long time, many years."

Chin's tidy revelation abruptly concluded the visit. They left almost immediately. Amy followed Corran back down the grass track to his hire car. Chin and Dao, someway ahead, left first. As Chin accelerated away, the rear end of his big German car slid out, an over-flamboyant swing that threw stones into the bushes, reflecting his utter contempt for the visit; time which could have been better spent between the sheets with his mistress in Khon Kaen.

Corran, turning the Toyota onto the main road, followed. As they drove away in silence, Amy pretended to look at the passing landscape. A line of monks walking at the edge of a paddy field provided the needed distraction. Taking in their flowing saffron robes and covered begging bowls, she stole a glance across the interior. Seeing Corran now sullenly back behind the wheel of the hire car, she was beginning to feel some sympathy for his situation; his humiliation at the hands of Dao and Chin had been especially galling. He looked crestfallen. But there was more than sorrow and pity behind her discomfort. She felt guilt.

It wasn't entirely correct what she had told Corran back at the hotel. Yes, it was true that she had bumped into Dao in the foyer of the hotel on his way out to collect Corran from the police station, but the chance meeting had developed into a deeper discussion. Dao had quickly understood Amy's pressing urgency to get Corran out of Chaiyaphum. She wanted the whole painful episode closed as much as he did. They were on the same side. Together, they had orchestrated the visit to the lakeside restaurant. Before Dao had gone onto the police station to meet Corran (keeping him there longer than was perhaps necessary by being over bureaucratic with the documents), he had called Chin, arranging for him to speak with Amy at the hotel to secure his acquiescence to the plan; a plan that in retrospect had been surprisingly effective.

Had that victory been too severe? Of course she knew there would be disappointment. But his reaction, considering the state of the place, had been extraordinary, surely excessive? She had no idea he'd be so affected by such a setback. Giving edge to her concerns was the thought of what was coming. The next two days were crucial. There was a conference call with the Lescari crowd (hopefully the last call they would need). She had to tread carefully, ensure he was back on side, didn't go off the rails. On top of that, there were the remaining gourmet guests to appease; a whole agenda of tuition sessions, speeches and a gala dinner to prepare. Was Corran up to it? Could he still impress as a celebrity chef?

Her tone softened.

"You never told me how this whole thing started?" she asked.

"What?" he replied, still vexed.

"If you had to go back to the beginning?"

"Beginning of what?"

"This whole restaurant thing."

"You really want to know?"

"Why not?"

"It was the truck jam. When I turned off the main highway."

"Show me."

Corran was suspicious. Ten minutes earlier, she had looked nothing but doubtful. Why would she want to go there? What was her purpose? Was she just placating, humouring him?

"I thought you didn't believe a word of what I was saying?"

"I never said that."

He glanced across as if to check her sincerity.

"It's about ten minutes away..."

"We can be quick."

Corran turned the car around. Finding the main road out of Chaiyaphum, he drove the now familiar route back to the main highway. They arrived at the cutting in the hillside where he had first encountered the line of sugarcane trucks. Parking up on the hard shoulder, they got out of the car. The route in both directions was empty and quiet. A strong warm wind blew up the valley. It howled around the scaffolding of the large billboard, producing a low, undulating whistle.

"This is where the jam started?" she asked.

"I came over that hill," he said, pointing up the incline.

"I was careless. On my mobile. Texting you actually. A truck was blocking the road. I slid into the back of it."

"You never told me you'd crashed."

"Crash might not be the right word. It was a shunt. A small one."

"Where did it happen?"

"Down there. By the fence post."

Amy walked down the hill. Reaching the marker, she scanned the road surface and saw pieces of the shattered left-side indicator from the front of Corran's hire car. A dark tyre-mark marred the tarmac. Returning back up the road to the Toyota, she knelt and felt the sharp edges of the broken indicator light. The front bumper was also deformed from the impact.

"You call it a small shunt, but you've smashed the side light and dented the bumper."

"Cheap Japanese for you. All foam and plastic."

Amy opened the driver's door. Leaning inside she scanned the interior. As with all hire cars, the dashboard, steering wheel and main controls were squeaky clean, almost 'delivery' new. She was examining the windscreen when a prominent mark on the surface caught her eye. She turned back to Corran.

"You must have hit the glass."

Instinctively he reached to his forehead. A bruise still remained. It had caused him some irritation on the first night, but headache pills had quickly dulled the throbbing pain. Since then he hadn't thought anymore about it.

She persisted: "How come you hit the screen?"

"I don't know."

"You had your seat belt on?"

"I might have taken it off... to reach for my phone."

She stepped closer to him; she could see a mark on his forehead above his eye. As she reached out to sweep his hair out of the way, he put his arm out, irritated by her solicitude.

"Oh c'mon Corran, I'm just having a look."

"It's nothing..."

"It looks like you had quite a knock."

"What does that mean?" he shot back.

"I mean you didn't mention it before. You don't think it might have had some kind of effect?"

"Effect? What are you suggesting?"

She shrugged, "Hitting the glass..."

"Made me see things, is that what you're getting at?"

"I don't know."

"Jeez..." he started walking away. "We're just wasting time."

"It's not unknown," she called after him.

He turned back to face her, his expression fierce.

"You really think that hitting my head on the windscreen, that small knock, somehow made me dream up this whole thing, that I imagined it?"

He was getting agitated again.

"I don't know. It could have. I'm not a doctor."

The drive back to Chaiyaphum was painful. Amy, avoiding eye contact, once again locked her eyes on the scenery – the fields, trees, villages and houses rushing by. Corran drove recklessly, without speaking or looking at her. Not that he was in any mood for conversation. Her suggestion that the small 'accident' on the hill might have affected his memory still riled him. He hated her doubt. She hadn't gone to the highway to help clear his mind and be understanding, she had gone there because she was suspicious, to prise out the holes in his story. Of course, she had always questioned him before. That was in her nature, partly why he had employed her in the first place; to cover his back, be critical, look for the gaps. But beneath it all there was always an unseen bond, an allegiance, a faith, that ultimately – once all the disagreements and petty squabbles were put aside – she still believed and trusted him. That faith had gone.

As they turned onto the main high street that led though the town, a second incident also disturbed him. A text came through on her mobile. Seeing who it was from, she had opened it quickly, angling the screen just a little more than was necessary to read the message. Normally brief in her correspondence, it had also taken her a long time to type out a reply. He pretended to ignore it.

Twenty Five

They got back to the hotel as the sun was falling. With few cars in the car park, Corran headed for a space next to the entrance. He came in at speed, stamping the brakes at the very last moment, nudging a concrete bollard, taking a chip out of it.

Amy followed him up the steps and through the double doors into the reception. Collecting his key, Corran continued across the hall.

"It's Andresen, isn't it?" said Corran.

"Andresen what?" she replied.

"You're leaving me to join that shit Andresen."

He had caught her off-guard. Her denial should have been quick, instinctive. But she was no good at lying.

"Can we talk about this?" she sighed.

"I knew it!" he hissed.

"Do you even check your messages?"

"That stream of junk from New York, you think I have time?"

"You didn't get Andresen's email then?"

"When?"

"Two days ago. If you'd bothered to read it, you'd know what this was all about."

"No, I didn't see it," he groaned.

"He's putting together something big in the States..."

She paused, making sure he was still listening. "It's not just me. He wants both of us."

"Both of us," he repeated, almost spitting the word, "We're not a dinner party item, husband and fucking wife," his bitterness with everyone, Amy to Andresen, getting the better of him.

"You're not even curious? Don't want to know what it's about?"

"No. Actually I'm not."

She shook her head. "What the hell is wrong with you, Corran? This is the biggest opportunity anyone could have in a lifetime. It's like flying to the moon, yet for some reason you're still wallowing about like some pig in a mud bath. Why? Why would you do that?"

"Because right now I can't take anymore. I can't think, I can't write, I can't do shit. And then this Andresen thing. Sure he's a smart guy. But ultimately he's just another fast-talking big-shot with yet another over-cooked deal that everyone will endlessly fuss over and then fuck up. I don't have the time or the patience for it. I don't have, don't know how... where I'll be in ten minutes... a year..."

He was speaking too fast, frustration and anger scrambling his thoughts, making his words slurred. She was suspicious.

"Wait a moment... You're not still..."

He looked awkward, ill at ease.

"...you're not still thinking about that place are you?"

Again he was hesitant.

"Unbelievable. We went there. It was a dump. There was nothing..."

"And you know why there was nothing?" Lowering his voice, he glanced warily down the hall. "Because those two, that slime-ball deputy manager and that poker-faced police shit, they're hiding something. They're as anxious as you to get me out of here. Why? Why the hell would they do that?"

"And why the hell should you care?"

"Something's going on. You can't see that?"

"No, I can't. But what I can see is that you're finding this hard, Corran, very hard. So let me spell it out, ABC style. There's a meeting planned with Andresen. Tomorrow. I need to know if you're going to be there. If the answer is yes, we need to leave now."

"I can't say right now."

"What?"

"I need more time..."

Amy broke a smile.

"Fine. That makes it simple."

"Simple?"

"I'm leaving you, Corran. Resigning. It's over."

She turned and walked away.

Corran, stunned, was left standing there. He hadn't foreseen this. He was forced to run after her.

"Wait!"

He caught up with her in the foyer.

"Amy, wait!"

She pulled away, tears running down her face.

"Let it go, Corran! Forget it. Can't you see? It's just another stupid place, another stupid recipe. You have thousands of them. From every country in the fucking world. It won't change anything!"

"No, Amy, you have to understand. It changes everything."

"Everything?"

"It makes a huge difference."

"And that difference will be the end of your career. Lescari are close to pulling the plug on you. If they pull the plug, they'll want their money back. And you'll be left staring at a pile of ashes that will only be of your own making. Yet another casualty of ego and fucked-up thinking. History is littered with them."

Twenty Six

Corran let Amy go. After the argument, she had left almost immediately. Needing time alone to think things through, he went up to his room. The cleaners were hoovering the floor. He shouted at them because they'd tidied his tabletop. Notes that he'd meticulously arranged in sequence had got mixed up, some had fallen behind the desk console.

Forgoing dinner, Corran left the hotel. Taking a side street adjacent to the entrance, he walked with no clear idea of where he was going or how long he would be gone.

Being mid-May and well into the monsoon, the appearance of dark clouds, wrapping themselves like giant wings around the outer fringes of the town, should have forewarned him of the coming storm. Minutes later the skies opened. Corran, without a rain jacket or hat, was yet again drenched. Not that he cared; the rain, heavy and angry, was like being battered by a thousand sadistic masseurs. He found the effect perversely calming, cooling his seething rage – rage at being unable to unearth the secrets of the restaurant, rage at not finishing the book, the bitter feud with Lescari, and now Amy walking out on him.

It was this last betrayal that hurt most. The shock that she had even entertained the idea of joining Andresen only enflamed his resentment. Who was he fooling with his hipster Hollister jeans and stone-washed T-shirts? Phoney was stamped over every molecule of his honed, triathlon physique. Maybe that was her secret craving – hanging with rich losers and loafers, a life of protein shakes, gluten – free cronuts and mocktails in members' only spas. And if that was the extent of her shallow ambition, then why the hell should he care? Move on. Wave goodbye. Fuck the ungrateful bitch!

Amy was nothing when he'd first met her. Although he'd told everyone they'd met on an international flight, in truth he'd bumped into her by chance at an internet cafe in Delhi. Unwashed and bedraggled, she was bent over a table, snivelling into her last napkin, ten minutes after her boyfriend had just dumped her to head to the airport and the comforts of his safe basement flat in Peckham. Starring blankly into the cracked screen of her mobile, her last pleading text had gone unanswered. She had no idea where she was going, where she would stay or how she would pay for her last miserable latte. It was just pity that had coerced Corran to give her a break. The job was almost meaningless – indexing pages for a small publication he'd already finished. Her willingness and enthusiasm, initially so ingratiating it had verged on the embarrassing, had persuaded Corran to let her help out with the last two weeks of his tour of Sikkim.

Still tender with heartbreak, she'd tagged along when he moved back to Sydney. From that moment on he had given her everything. Taught her all there was to know about his profession, introduced her to the crucial contacts and provided the guidance. Without him, without his name on the entry card, she'd still be pushing coffee and stale biscuits at some grubby internship. Every step she'd made up the greasy ladder of PR, he'd been the one holding both the steps and her hand. In time she'd come to realise that. After two, or three weeks of dealing with Andresen's wearisome drudgery, regrets were sure to follow.

A dull wooden echo intruded from a side street. Hollow, almost theatrical, it was like the sound of a grovelling knock on a door. Gleefully, he imagined a sad, solitary figure on the threshold of his harbour-side apartment, wretched, in tears, on her knees – Amy, begging for her job back. In his mind he played through how he would answer, if he would even answer. Did he still need her? Why? When there were hundreds, thousands more eager and qualified queuing at his door?

No. It was over. There was no going back. That chapter was closed, nailed shut, buried and grassed over.

Six months ago he had been entered into *Time* magazine's list of one hundred of the most influential people on the planet. Although the final selection was peppered with mostly underserving, 'bright young things' purely to spice up its viral appeal, there were also names that Corran respected – the journalist, Charlie Rose, and the activist chef, Alice Brice Walters. Squeezing him in at ninety-seven, *Time* had praised Corran's vision of an all-embracing shared world culture, food bringing communities together, breaking down barriers, fostering exchange and understanding. Eschewing the hegemony of the faceless multi-nationals and global brands, he had expounded upon his vision for a sharing economy that embraced equality and the power of crowds. A rare egalitarian outburst that was comfortably in print and nested before his million-dollar deal with Lescari had been banked. Of course, on reflection, although it caused him some pain at this particular juncture to admit it, a small slice of that success had been Amy's.

The founding idea for the book had always been his. He'd kept notes on the subject for the last five years. That was indisputable. But yes, if someone had forced his fingers into a meat grinder and he was impelled to give her some credit, he would have had to concede that she had, in her own small way, been useful, even resourceful. She had been the one who had pushed the ambition and scale of the project, even coming up with the title, *The Story of Food*. Naturally, most of that was down to the fact that he'd had the foresight to trust her and give her free rein in the first place. And running with it she had done well. It would be disingenuous to suggest otherwise. Not only had she tied up the contract with Lescari, she had secured the Netflix series and organised the worldwide distribution. Luck had something to do with it. And his name, his 'brand', Corran Brook, had always carried her across the more difficult divides. After all, the commodity she was shifting wasn't canned air – it was his talent, his recipes, his creations, his magic.

Corran, reached a crossroads and heard the uneven growl of an approaching diesel engine. He was forced to stop. A garbage truck rounded the corner. As the lorry passed by it hit a puddle. Corran, still embroiled within his turbulent battles, was slow to react. A wall of water rose up in a wave and splashed across his face. The slap was a shock, killing his internal ramblings. As he stepped out from the shadows, a more corrupting narrative had time to intrude. It emerged from a dismal cavity in his psyche and, as he wiped the dirt from his face, sneaked a front seat in his consciousness: He was wrong.

The reality, the unpalatable, irritating truth he had been desperately trying to smother and kill, was that if he'd really looked honestly at all the output that he had achieved over the recent past – from television shows, publishing and the opening of new restaurants – it had been Amy who had been making the critical difference. It was her thinking, her insights, her initiatives that had injected the necessary vitality into ideas and projects that were at best, moribund, 'also ran'.

Slowly, the corrosive idea that Amy might have been right, that he was being a complete fool, seeped into the limelight. Overshadowed by this change in perspective, he felt diminished. His sense of himself on the world stage, like retreating armies on a board game, fell back on a diminishing fiefdom of one.

Sometimes vanity, like an uninvited beast that holds forth at dinner parties, can take to the comfy armchair by the fire and become your permanent friend. A stay-at-home vice rather than a visitor.

What was he really? Rich, sure. Hard working, yes. Disciplined, most of the time. Inspired? That was where his virtues entered unknown territory. Certainly no one would rank him a great thinker. His talent – too strong a word – his vocation, was more that of the thief. Yet even that dismal reading of his condition hadn't even been his own insight. A food critic, Jack Klein, had reached that painful conclusion six months before in an agonising review of his television show, "Food Crazy", on NBC. The words 'flabby, 'crass', and 'vacuous' had been the kinder adjectives. The critic had accused Corran of unashamedly copying everything – the format, style and design of the programme – from a little known cable channel in South Korea. He had even used the same font in his title sequence. Ok, Klein's profile was ridiculously small, his readership, especially online, laughable compared to his own, but the damage to Corran's fragile, sensitive soul had been seismic. And yet again (finding himself being dragged once more to the confessional), it was Amy, who, after threatening Klein with litigation, had ensured that the damaging blog post was taken down, saving his reputation.

Corran turned the corner of a street and found himself by chance back at the centre of the now-deserted food market. The wooden stalls and concrete walkways looked grey and grubby in the pouring rain. In fact he was only yards from the very position in which he had last seen the girl. As his eyes focused on the spot, the recall of her last movements across the tarmac played back through his memory with painful clarity. He could see her clearly now – her pale face, her jet black hair, her bright golden eyes. It wasn't the old woman he had followed. It was her.

Corran stumbled forward, dragging his feet through the deep puddles, as if being closer to the place he had last seen her might afford him a better view. It had the opposite effect; the vision clouded and the movie in his mind dulled and finally extinguished. The car park, now empty of taxis, scooters and buses, was just one large dirty expanse of mud and water.

For seconds, Corran was disorientated. How had he got there? Why on earth had he returned? Was he so miserably intoxicated by romantic fantasies that he had subconsciously walked back to the market in the forlorn hope of seeing her again?

Twenty Seven

The River Grand was the largest of several high-profile, luxury eco-hotels that had carved out a position on the banks of the Mekong river in Nong Khai. Jointly owned by a Singaporean venture-capital firm, Imperial First, it was built on land previously occupied by a failing bungalow lodge, The Silver Sands Retreat. The lodge was owned by an American, Herbert Miller, who had stayed on in the area after the Vietnam War. Formerly a flight mechanic, who worked on B52's and ageing DC 5's, he had married a Thai wife and opened a cafe at the Udon Airbase, 25 miles south of Nong Khai. The airbase was famous for being the operational headquarters of the CIA's clandestine airline, Air America, set up to fly covert missions over Laos during the conflict. As well as ferrying spies, diplomats and special forces into the war zone, it also flew in 'rice drops', mercy missions of food supplies to villages whose crops had been destroyed by the American's over-zealous use of the defoliant, Agent Orange. 'Hard Rice' – bullets, grenades, shells and guns for the US-backed Hmong tribesmen – was also part of the aid mix.

With so much tonnage going in and so little coming back, idle minds speculated on how best to fill the empty transports returning home. It was alleged that opium was part of this trade, a rumour fiercely denied by the US government. An investigation initiated by

Washington was inconclusive; besides the war was almost over.

By the time the airline had closed down in the late 1970's, Herbert Miller and his Thai wife had amassed an unexpected fortune from their coffee-shop operation, enough for them to build a 100-room hotel complex on a prime site on the river – the first with air-conditioning in each room, together with hot tubs from the original Jacuzzi company.

They had managed the Silver Sands for close to three decades. Run on a shoestring, occupancy had never been high. Miller, seeing his lifetime's ambition slowly being eaten away by termites and damp, surrendered control to his only daughter, May. After four years at business school in Singapore, she was more than capable. Financially astute and commercially minded, May had a keen eye for the numbers, the highest being the value of the land. To celebrate the hotel's thirtieth birthday, she sent her parents on an extended beach holiday in the Andaman Islands and called in the bulldozers. With her contacts from business school she had pieced together an investment deal with a Singaporean banking group. The new building, designed by a young Dutch architect, was constructed in a minimalist Scandinavian style – untreated woods, open courtyards and facades of natural stone. After completion, with her parents safely lodged in a small bungalow on the fringes of the estate (the only building preserved from the original Silver Sands), May had stayed on to jointly manage the hotel.

W Lux were one of the first tour groups to use the hotel as a 'base camp' from which they could coordinate their regional expeditions. Using a private flight company in Udon, flying leased, 70-seater, ATR turbo props, they were able to shuffle their high-paying clients around the rarer, 'off-the-beaten-track' highlights of Southeast Asia – from hidden jungle temples beyond Angkor, mountain villages in the Northern Shan States, to riding the tea-horse trail in Yunnan.

A specialist arm of W Lux organised the Gourmet Food Experience, a mixed programme that combined tours of ancient cultural sites with culinary insights from some of the world's most famous chefs.

The current tour group, consisting of guests from Europe, America, Canada and Japan, had arrived at the hotel after a four-day cruise down the Mekong from the ancient Laotian capital, Luang Prabang. Initially underwhelmed and feeling slightly abandoned after their star chef had failed to materialise, they had had their faith in their high-end experience restored, when Corran had put in two full and intense days of virtually private tuition. He had driven them to remote villages, had them planting rice in paddy fields, and guided them through local food markets, whilst providing rare insights into Thailand's ingredients and spices (knowledge he'd shamelessly recycled from Timi's 'Auntie' in the Chaiyaphum market).

It hadn't all gone smoothly. After their boat had broken down while fishing for catfish, they had mistakenly strayed across the border line (difficult to discern on shifting waters) and were arrested by a Laotian militia. Corran had had to use the last of his one-thousand baht bills, together with their precious river catch, to bribe local officials to ferry them back across the divide.

Corran's great efforts had culminated in an afternoon in the kitchens where they had prepared dishes for their last evening meal – spicy rock lobster with papaya and star fruit, was followed by seaweed tempura and *moo ping douro*, pieces of pork marinated in coconut milk, lemon grass and madeira. The evening commenced with a talk given by Corran on the subject of food and the future frontiers of cuisine.

Corran touched on the true trailblazers of the past decade: Eneko Atxa of the hillside restaurant, Azurmendi near Bilbao; Andre Chiang from Restaurant Andre, Singapore; and Eshen Holmboe Bang, from Maaemo in Norway. From new ingredients to techniques and styles of cooking, these were the rare talents who were transforming the dining experience, and shaking up a discipline that was in danger of becoming narcissistic and moribund. This handful of stars were the true explorers and risk-takers; the rest – all the pretenders and sycophants – were just camp followers and stragglers.

The talk was enthusiastically received. The audience of silver-haired 'sixty somethings' made a surprisingly unruly clamour, appreciatively clapping and stamping their Birkenstock-clad feet. Corran was coerced back to the stage. With typically British-style self-deprecation, he played down their accolades. No leading light or visionary guru, he was ok being placed within the ranks of the second wave, 'the camp followers' and 'bag handlers', one stop short of the fakers and flaneurs. His brilliance was nothing without his exceptional crew. And he made a big song and dance about introducing the 'prime mover' within his team, "the young, brilliant and beautiful, Amy Carlyle."

After the talk, the tour group was invited outside for cocktails. Tables covered with pristine white tablecloths and lit by candle-light had been laid out overlooking the river. Large lanterns hung from the lower branches of a mango tree. The aged Herbert Miller, needing a sturdy stick to navigate the uneven laterite walkways, also put in an appearance with his young director and daughter, May.

Corran made the rounds, dutifully pausing at each table of guests to hear out their tales and experiences. A rogue elephant had got loose on the riverside promenade. Two Canadians had bought carvings from a lost Polynesian tribe that turned out to be fake (few can disguise the scent of burnt charcoal). A young couple from Seoul, newly married, had discovered a scorpion in their lunch box, an inauspicious sign for Korean families.

Not all was high drama. There were more prosaic questions to answer from the afternoon in the kitchen – how to grind spices, de-bone a cat-fish, cooking times for quail. Corran, listening patiently to their queries and problems, dispensed his culinary wisdom with quiet authority, as if revealing trade secrets known only to a few.

A middle-aged couple from Utah were planning a caravan trip across Queensland. Uncharacteristically Corran gave them his direct line and an open invitation to visit.

Cocktails led on to the meal that the four teams had prepared earlier. Being the last day of their schedule, the hotel had planned a spectacular finale. Local craftsmen had built a traditional grass village in the front garden. Two miniature Vietnamese pot-bellied pigs, scrubbed and cleaned every morning with shower-gel, were brought in on a pick-up truck. The restaurant waitresses dressed up in Isarn folk costume and skirts. The waiters wore rough cotton *chong kraben* and woven reed sandals.

Across the water a horn sounded. Appearing on a bend of the Mekong, a troupe of dancing girls came down-river in wooden canoes. As they stepped ashore, local musicians on stringed instruments and reed flutes struck up an eerie tune that sounded like stray cats being taunted. To a second fanfare of horns, the main dishes appeared on the back of an ox cart decorated with palm branches and orchids.

After the meal, the cooking awards were presented. Acting as ring master and grand jury, Corran delivered accolades and praise to virtually every member of the team, regardless of talent. Even the most inept attempt – a sprawling mess of burnt pork, scorched vegetables and puffed, over-cooked noodles – received a special consolation prize of an intricately carved wooden duck, that would no doubt adorn a crowded mantelpiece back home in West Virginia, a talking point when the conversation lulled. Speeches were made, fireworks set off and lantern balloons launched to fill the night sky.

It was already dark when Amy caught up with Corran.

"Can I steal him from you?" she asked of the guests.

"No you can't," the silver haired ladies replied, "We want to take him home."

Corran made his apologies to those at the table. Finishing his champagne, he posed for one last group shot, before Amy pulled him away.

"Nice smile, Corran. One more, you'll be trending on Instagram, hashtag "cheesy faces," she whispered.

"Just keeping the campers happy..." he replied.

"You've made lifelong friends. I hope you've got plenty of spare beds."

They continued across the garden.

"Andresen has just got in. He wants to meet," she said.

"What, now? Seriously? You originally said six?"

"That's what I was told. They had problems getting here. But hopefully, being so late, it won't take long. They'll want to crash out."

"I have to warn you, I'm in no fit state to say anything smart."

"I'm not asking you to talk, Corran, just listen."

Reaching the end of the garden, they entered the back of the hotel. Crossing the hall, they had trouble getting into the foyer; the entrance hallway was clogged with suitcases and trunks. It turned out to be Andresen's personalised luggage. A small convoy of four-wheel drive trucks had brought them in from the airport. Rich people had a lot of baggage, Corran reflected. What was it that they moved around with them all over the world? Surely more than just clothes?

Seconds later, Andresen strolled through the double doors. Still dressed in the same freshman-style jeans and T-shirt he had last seen him wear in Bangkok, he wrapped his arms around Corran as if he had known him for years. Favia also kissed him and gave a comforting hug. But she was more interested in Amy. Anxious to show her pictures she had taken in Cambodia, they took the lift to her suite on the top floor.

"I need a drink," said Andresen, fielding a call from California and guiding Corran through the swing doors to the bar.

Twenty Eight

Andresen, crossing the bar, brought out a small bottle of whisky he had stashed in his luggage – Sullivan's Cove, a rare Tasmanian single malt (typically, only 516 bottles had ever been produced and Andresen had half of them). He led Corran to an armchair arranged on a large veranda overlooking the Mekong. The moon, flickering through the palm trees on the Laotian side, reflected in the silently shifting waters of the great river.

Andresen apologised for missing Corran's talk. They had just flown in from Siem Riep late in the afternoon. The last half hour of the approach had been rough. Storm clouds had collected over the mountain ranges. At one point the pilot, uncertain whether they'd be able to land at Udon at all, had called the control tower. Commercial flights were being turned away. They dropped altitude hoping for calmer conditions, but on the descent the weather became more turbulent. Of course, the jet was equipped to use autoland, but the signals from the ILS antennas at Udon were weak – narrow-beam transponders that had remained unchanged since the war. Andresen, from birth a nervous flyer and worried about the efficacy of his twenty-one ton toy, had wanted to call it a day and turn back to Cambodia. It was Favia, trusting in the ability of her Austrian flight crew to fly almost blind through anything, who had been the one to persist.

Favia had planned the trip to the temples at Angkor Wat to coincide with a symposium she wanted to attend in Siem Reap on Khmer archaeology. Anxious that the presence of coach tours might despoil her appreciation of the ancient sites, she had organised a private group to visit some of the newly-discovered and only partially excavated temples.

A number of prominent academics, giving papers at the symposium, had been invited. Although obviously erudite in their chosen areas of expertise – one was a hydraulics engineer, another a reader of inscriptions and bas reliefs – Andresen had found their narrow-minded focus on their specialist fields of knowledge, self-serving, even fetishistic. No one had the grand world vision, the wider picture. Defensive and possessive over their small islands of learning, they bickered.

Over two days of travel, these academic jealousies and rivalries, had, like scum on a chicken broth, boiled to the surface. Bitter back-seat disputes had broken out over window seats, whether the air-conditioning should be on or off and who should be chosen to sit in the more comfortable lead vehicle. And then there was the food – simple village restaurants found themselves being interrogated by anxious vegetarians, pescatarians and those with allergies to gluten, shell fish and MSG.

Andresen, desperate for an escape, had bought a local guidebook from a street stall and, to the concern of the drivers and guides, had intentionally lost himself in the ruins. Their concerns were real; there were still unexploded land mines from the war (alarming red signs inscribed with the words, 'Nguy Hiem' dotted the jungle paths), mosquitoes the size of small wasps and plenty of venomous snakes. Andresen, brushing away the concerns and relieved to have escaped the laborious monologues of the academics, had soaked up the silence. Contemplating stacks of stones wrapped up in hundreds of years of undergrowth, half-strangled by twisted tree roots and ferns, he had let his mind wander.

Sites such as Angkor hide many narratives. Some see stories about wars and religion, architecture and art, geology and erosion, birds and bugs. Others see numbers, the veracity of data, the accuracy of dates, the weights of carvings and stones. But Andresen saw only ideas.

What is it with thinking? Why do some people wake up in the morning and make a cheese omelette, whilst others wake up and decide to build an empire? And for their lifetime that's what they do, followed by the next generation thereafter. For hundreds of years they build these vast, intricate and beautiful temples in the middle of nowhere. And then one day, 'boom' – it's all over, they go and never come back. But the buildings, the statues and the inscriptions remain, edifices that will endure for possibly centuries to come.

That's what interested Andresen – legacy. It was constructs like these that brought about the big changes. Concepts so powerful that they don't just endure, they form the stepping stones for civilisations to follow.

"Look, Corran, I want to be straight with you. I could yack on about websites, smart apps and augmented realities. But that's a ten-minute conversation. And to be honest, despite what you might read about me online, that doesn't interest me. But if that's where you're heading, fine. We can finish our drink, part as friends and move on."

"That would be a shame," replied Corran, anxious not to pass on an opportunity to sample such a renowned malt. "We should at least finish the bottle".

Andresen poured him another glass. "One more for the road then."

"What road?" questioned Corran.

Twenty Nine

It was a shock to hear that Andresen had hired two mountain bikes (he'd even organised lycra cycling shorts). It was way past twelve, the dinner on the veranda long over, his tour group safely in bed.

Ten minutes later, the two of them were weaving between scooters and pick-up trucks on the Rim Kong highway out of Nong Khai.

Andersen professed to be one of that new breed of thinkers who liked to get out, believing that being outside and having exercise 'opened minds' and encouraged people to talk more freely and candidly. Although, for most of the ride, as Corran struggled with the pace and the unfamiliar gear shifts, the athletic American did most of the talking.

Andresen rewound back twenty years. Curiously he didn't dwell as long on his accomplishments as his failures. He had lost a fortune on the first internet "revolution". Having recklessly taken money from friends and family, he had backed a Facebook-like social network, before Facebook. A year too early in the media's evolution, it had been a spectacular and salutary disaster, one of the first to join the ninety-nine percent club (Internet floats that lost ninety-nine percent of their value). Courting personal bankruptcy, he had been forced to sell his San Francisco Bay apartment and take his kids out of private school to pay back his creditors. His wife of fifteen years, unable to face the shame of a return to humble austerity, left him and went back to her family in Sweden (endearingly to return to a pre-school sweetheart, now a drummer in a band).

Despite these early setbacks, Andresen had clung tenaciously to four stock-holdings that had grown to become the now-familiar global household names, known by the acronym, Gafa: Google, Apple, Facebook and Amazon. And when others had run for the hills, he had ploughed what remained of his business into software for mobiles. He derided those who claimed that the main tech empires were already established and built. In his mind they were just the raw foundations. We were still in the unthinking, mindless, 'dumb', even Neanderthal stage. A new land grab was yet to be realised. A revolution that was a hundred times more advanced, intelligent and radical.

Take Corran's own discipline, food. Yes there were hundreds of millions of websites online. Corran had his own resource. And compared to other famous chefs, his results were high – half a million visitors in the last month alone. But such sites were still delivering glorified library pages, pages that had to be found, linked to and read. How you prepared a meal, the ingredients you bought, the recipes you followed, had remained unchanged since the first Roman recipe book, *De re Coquinaria*, compiled by the original gourmet, Marcus Apicius, more than two thousand years ago (a reference that Corran had used in his own lectures – maybe Andresen really had read his book). Yet, Andresen continued, the whole business of food, the financial rewards and the power still accrued to a handful of global conglomerates.

They were reaching the edge of Nong Khai. Rows of thin townhouses gave way to open fields and plains. As the town receded, so too did the comfort of street lamps and soon they were cycling with only the weak beams from their bike lights to guide them. On their right-hand side, sand-banks and islands on the river could be seen through the palm trees. They passed a group of traditional Thai houses. Lying in the dirt under the teak stilts, a gang of dogs rushed out. The threat of getting a mauling gave Corran the necessary incentive to speed up.

"What if there was a better way?" asked Andresen casually, as if he were pondering a sudoku puzzle.

"That our entire relationship with food and drink could be transformed? That there was a system that knew and cared for you better than your mother, or girlfriend. A system that would be designed to fight your corner, that would be there 24/7 for your benefit and advantage."

Andresen paused, as if to let a child catch up – as indeed he had to – both physically and mentally. For Corran, too tired to fully absorb the immensity of Andresen's import, was still several chapters and metres behind. The thought of a king-sized bed with crisp Egyptian cotton sheets, an orchid and a square of Cailler chocolate on the pillow had something to do with it. Of course, he knew the tech billionaire was a deal maker. That came with the territory. When Amy had called him into Andresen's presence, he had expected the great man to throw down some kind of gauntlet. Nothing too extraordinary or taxing – produce an online food show, be the judge on a cooking competition, make a celebrity appearance on one of his many cable outfits. But the scale of Andresen's thinking, like some fantastical ship that had suddenly emerged out of the mist, left Corran baffled. He could see the outline of masts, maybe some vague rigging, but what was below deck, let alone the vagaries of its captain, remained a mystery. Struggling for something coherent, material, he had no idea whether he was seeing madness or genius. Maybe that was Andresen's way – to soft talk the momentous as nonchalantly as if he were chatting about tennis. He had to stall him.

"Andresen, you're going way too fast. You're going to have to slow down."

"My pace is too quick?"

"Everything is too quick."

His plea saw Andresen reach for his brakes. He even shifted down a gear as a concession. Taking his eye off the road in front, he turned in his seat and looked back to Corran as if addressing the back of the class.

"Ok... let me try this another way."

They were passing through a small village on the river. Above the restaurants and bars on both sides of the road, billboards for soft drinks, snacks and hot noodle soups shone out with happy, pretty, expectant faces.

Andresen pointed to a promotion as they passed.

"Adverts and magazines shout out for our attention – this is good, this is healthy, this will make you more beautiful, thinner, sexier. Obviously we know its all baloney – an adman's wet dream, a lifestyle delusion invented by commerce. So, what if we junk it?"

"Junk what?" replied Corran, fumbling to correct a misaligned derailleur.

"Everything we've known about food. What we eat, how we eat, when we eat. No more cultural prescriptions. We start with a clean sheet."

"And that clean sheet is?", asked Corran skeptically.

"We call it nutritional synthesis."

There was a pause as Andresen reconsidered his last sentence.

"Although, hearing that now sounds like bullshit. We need something less verbose, more human..."

"You mean like GM?"

"That's a starting point. Though it gets way more complicated than that."

A dark shape broke from a bush and darted across the road. Corran braked to avoid it – some kind of weasel with white stripes on its bushy tail.

"Essentially everyone is born with a gene profile. Such a blueprint can tell you from birth, not only what food types are good for you, but also which ones will provide the right energy. It will know your metabolism, what health conditions you are susceptible to, what times of day you should be eating, even which foods should be taken for different physical and mental states. Your plate would look radically different depending on whether you were skiing down the Matterhorn, repositioning the space telescope, or painting the Mona Lisa."

"Doesn't it take the fun out of it?"

"If you're young and carefree and want a life of recreational sex and wild abandon, of course, it could match you to such a lifestyle. We're all for freedom of choice," he shrugged.

"Happiness guru, nutritionist and health coach rolled into one. It wouldn't bug you?" Corran cut in.

They'd reached the top of a hill. Andresen, standing on his pedals, sped up for the downhill run.

"Guidance. But not a nagging voice," shouted Andresen over his shoulder as he accelerated down.

Corran, pausing to catch his breath and relieve the burning sensations in his calf muscles, watched him go. His aching limbs were the least of his problems. The spirits, specifically the Tasmanian malt, still dulled his senses. His companion's discourse only added to his state of discombobulation.

Peering down the hill through the murky shadows, he could make out Andresen's silhouette. He had reached the bottom of the hill and was looking back over his shoulder, arms energetically waving for Corran to join him.

Of course, Andresen was encouraging him to imitate his own fast and reckless descent. But Corran, restrained by a fleeting image of his tangled body implanted head first in a water-logged paddy field, sat back in his seat and gently freewheeled.

Even that sedate pace wasn't easy. The surface of the road was pitch black, impossible to read. As he picked up speed, his eyes wavered between wide-eyed vigilance for potholes (some alarmingly deep) and fighting to avoid having his corneas peppered by clouds of small flies. Trusting to luck, he closed his eyes. It was a bad idea. Lulled by the soft, languid breeze, his mind started to drift into a dreamlike state that saw him gently floating above a sea of soft cloud and glinting stars. He was seconds away from completely shutting down, when his front wheel hit a sharp rut in the tarmac. The frame of his bicycle, bounced off the lip of the trench, propelling him several feet into the air. As the wheels slammed back to the road, his head was thrown forward, grazing his front teeth on the headset. Shaken back to reality, Corran had only seconds to make a sharp correction and avoid plunging over the edge of the road into a distant river bed. He managed to regain control, but a harsh vibration from the front forks revealed that he must have wrecked the shocks.

It took him some time to catch up with Andresen, now casually pulling out into the road to allow him time to come back alongside.

As Corran approached, brushing back the hair that had fallen over his forehead, the tech billionaire's dialogue continued, oblivious to the obvious interlude and the erratic squealing sound from his damaged front forks.

"...less dictatorial, more a nudge, an influence that would inform every aspect of your life, your wellbeing and your work. Such an advance would have profound social benefits. You'd be fitter, never be overweight, defend yourself naturally against common illnesses and more importantly, you'd be smarter. Way smarter. Though we're not just doing this to breed Wall Street bankers. This is a vision for the world. To both feed people, and make them healthier, more intelligent, without fucking up the planet."

The road had opened up. Following the banks of the river, the bends of the highway ebbed and flowed like the contours of a kids' skateboard park. Andresen once again shifted down and moving ahead, let his bike flow gracefully into the dips and curves.

Corran, again back of the pack, had time to reflect. Shaken out of his dazed inebriation by his near fatal crash, it was starting to make sense. And, although he was still dazzled by the sheer audacity of Andresen's utopian thinking, Corran could see it was a big deal. A really big deal. It was the sort of grand vision thing that Renaissance artists painted on the underside of large cathedral copulas, replete with towering clouds, angels, cherubs and shafts of enlightenment.

As the road flattened out, Corran once again drew parallel with Andresen, the American's bike now free-wheeling, smartphone balanced on the handlebars as he checked his GPS.

"It can be done?" enquired Corran, softening the line to hide the doubt in his voice.

"It is done" Andresen answered with blithe, irritating simplicity, eyes still scanning his screen.

Corran had known his fair share of tech billionaires in his life. Most had just winged it and been lucky. With no special talent or contribution, they'd been in the right place at the right time, usually hanging out, Budd beer and burger in hand, by the barbecue. One had even been a pool-cleaning attendant. Though often slow-witted and a touch dim, their saving grace was that they had had the astuteness to say 'yes' when others, wary of risk, had backed away and said 'no'. And when their small start-ups had bounced through seed finance to venture capital with their merry-go-rounds of investment and inevitable dilution, they had quietly bided their time, avoiding boardroom battles and clashes of egos, until the all-important payout – the IPO.

Andresen was of a different breed. He was one of those rare types that showed true mastery over their actions. Many people can dream up ideas. But few have the willpower and fortitude to bridge that gaping chasm between nice insight and grand empire. Such minds are possessed of a mesmerising and sometimes quixotic charisma, a power over others that has remained unchanged over millennia. Like Xerxes at the Hellespont or Caesar on the Rubicon, Andresen was staring over that same kind of divide and showing no doubt, knew no fear.

For Corran, a single question remained. If Andresen saw himself as empire builder, where would he fall – high priest or spear carrier?

Andresen turned off the main road down a small track. On both sides lay pineapple groves skirted by tamarind trees.

"It sounds incredible. Unbelievable even. But if you can do all this, why the hell would you need me, where would I fit in?" asked Corran.

Andresen hit the flattery button, "No one has the depth of expertise or understanding that you do. Beyond the art of cooking, you know about people, culture and context. You know the emotional value of food. That's the knowledge base I want to build on. Without that, this project is all digits, black and white, without the colour, without the passion. We need someone who can tell our story, get under their skin, change behaviours."

As the track thinned, the sand got deeper and they were forced to dismount and push their bikes. It looked like they were heading towards the river. Small fruit bats flew overhead. Above the distant hills, he recognised the constellation of Orion and the line of misty stars that marked out its distinctive belt.

For seconds Corran was silent, his mind distracted both by the unexpected serenity of his surroundings and the immensity of what he had to grasp. He was being handed the keys to the kingdom and yet he was wary. Distrust was etched in his nature. Ever since graduation and his mauling by the duplicitous Lucy Mecker, feelings of elation and joy were often tainted with a certain foreboding and doubt. Was this for real, was it believable? How long had he known the guy? Less than a week. Check out Andresen online. There was bad press as well as good. Hadn't one of his companies been linked to a loan from a Panamanian Trust? Wasn't there talk of an FBI investigation?

Of course, he was overdoing it, his suspicions, accented by the late hour and the alcohol, overplayed. In reality, Andresen had looked nothing but earnest. Indeed, he'd been impressive, delivering his pitch with consummate skill and passion, albeit from the saddle of a mountain bike.

"Well?" checked Andresen, turning back to him.

"I'm flattered, Andresen. I had to double-check if it was really me you were talking to. Right now, I'm honoured just to be having this conversation. But you have to understand, this is a big deal, maybe the biggest I've ever encountered. I've only met you twice, you don't know me and, quite frankly, some of the stuff you talk about freaks me out. In a good way, you understand".

"Don't get me wrong. I'm not looking for an answer immediately. You need to sleep on it. But just to help you with your decision-making, let me sketch out a few details. You'll be the creative director. You dictate your own budget and terms, hire whoever you want, and on our side we'll deliver an office in whichever world capital you choose to base yourself. Money is not an issue. It's nothing to the cultural and social change we can bring about. Put simply, this is the biggest and most ambitious project I've ever launched. We want you on board."

Corran was beginning to fathom where Andresen was coming from. He'd done wealth. He'd been through the absurd yachts, the private jets, the beachfront mansions and the ranches. He was after a Medici moment, to have his proud mug carved in the monument that was humanity. This was the moonshot Amy had alluded to. A grand gesture to enter the history books.

Corran reflected on his own paltry endeavours, his years of research, his travels and his writing. What did he have to show for it? A small chain of restaurants, some dusty TV shows and a handful of books; mere castles in the sand compared to the epic pyramids that would be Andresen's legacy.

"What about Amy?" he asked.

"We want Amy too. She's a really important part of this thing. I mean, you've worked with her and obviously know how bright she is. You'll be a team. She'll head the division, deal with all the management issues and report back to the board. And as such, you'll get the same share ownership and the same option structure".

Amy was coming in on the same package as himself. That was a shock. No wonder she'd been so distant, so offhand in Chaiyaphum. Andresen had obviously already offered her the job. If she'd been asked first, did that mean that he was secondary? Had she betrayed his errant behaviour in the south? Had there been doubts? There were hundreds of talents worldwide comparable to his. In reality, he'd be easy to replace.

He heard voices. Looking through the trees, he could see a pontoon silhouetted against the glittering moonlit river. People had collected on the platform. Music was playing. Some were dancing. He even recognised the tune – a Nashville singer, Geena North. An obscure choice in somewhere so remote. And at this time of night, the last thing he expected.

The path came to a crossroads. With some relief he could see a sign pointing back the way they had come. It had to be the limit of the ride. Tugged by tiredness, he was absentmindedly straying in that direction when a shout from Andresen arrested him.

"Corran!"

He turned.

"I want you to meet some people."

"Great..."

Corran answered blandly, without thought. But then the anxiety sunk in. What did that mean? When, where?

"Now?"

"Look, I know you're tired. And I apologise for the terrible timing. But the flight from Angkor has totally messed up the evening. And I really want you to meet the team."

Surely they were in the middle of nowhere?

Corran turned and saw Andresen heading towards the river and the pontoon. As the music boomed once again from the distance, Corran realised with horror that the party on the raft, far from being boisterous locals, were 'the team'.

Thirty

Dragging his bike through the sand, Corran followed Andresen across the river bank to the edge of the water. A bamboo causeway had been constructed out from the shore to a wooden platform on which up to fifty people had gathered. Red paper lanterns, rattled by the breeze, lit the way. Hanging from tall posts, ghostly *Khon* spirit masks made from rice husks and coconut matting gave the scene a languid bohemian air. Beer, spirits and cocktails crowded a side table. A set of old wooden speakers were rigged to a set of iPhones – it was set up like a high school beach party.

Although Corran recognised one or two people from his talk, most of those on the pontoon, especially the younger group stretched out on large silk cushions facing Laos, he didn't know. Of course there was Amy. She was on the far side of the platform, too busy chatting to register his arrival. Back at the hotel she hadn't wasted time with Favia looking at photos; it was wardrobes they had shared and exchanged. In such a short space of time (in fact since their first meeting in Bangkok), he was surprised, if not a little wary, to see how close they had become. Amy, who only days earlier had been his humble 'do anything' assistant, now hitched up in a Donna Karen shirt and lace skirt, cut the profile of a daunting executive.

"I didn't recognise you in designer guise," said Corran approaching her.

"I didn't recognise you in Lycra."

He glanced down at his cycle shorts; they looked tight and a touch absurd in the setting.

"Careful, you're in danger of getting fit."

Her remark needled him; was she suggesting he was 'unfit', needing exercise? Amy, typically, was a health fanatic, one more area of prowess where she clearly outshone him with the ever-competitive Americans.

"Perhaps we could arrange for a running machine in the boardroom?"

"I thought you wanted a whisky bar?" she shot back with mischievous intent.

Andresen, sensing the friction, steered Corran on a course to some fresher faces.

Leaning casually against a handrail at the entrance to the raft was a young Danish man, Kurt Christian. Kurt was Andresen's CFO. Lean, tanned, blonde, wearing flowery beach-bum shorts as if he had just navigated the length of the Mekong on a paddle board, Kurt was as laid-back as a sunset over Maui. Peppering his conversation with talk of peaks, swells, cutbacks and breaks, it took Corran a while to realise he was speaking about finance.

Kurt was legendary at Harvard at a time when geniuses were being cranked out with almost every semester. In his first year, when he had spent most of his time climbing obscure mountain peaks, he had stumbled on an algorithm that tied weather conditions with movements on stock indices. The idea was based on the theory that clear skies or rain often impacted on sentiment and thus investor behaviour. The idea wasn't entirely new. His insight was context. Single days of sun or rain made little impact. It was the frequency and depth of weather events matched to news volatility that chimed; a composite picture of gloom or elation.

With no money to his name, Kurt had invested with his own meagre earnings, savings from a holiday job delivering sushi on a scooter. After two years and a summer of spectacular bad weather events across the

US (exacerbated by a particularly fierce El Nino), his rolling equity had grown sufficiently to pay for his tuition fees. Turning his attention to China and the Far East, where such anomalies had an even more pronounced effect on mood swings, his gains had been large enough to secure a down payment on a modest beach shack in Malibu.

Naturally, word had got out. A prominent Boston hedge fund had beaten a path to his door. Slyly selecting negotiators who were also keen surfers, they had holed up in a hired Winnebago on the beach in an attempt to engineer a chance meeting. Bouncing into Kurt amid the waves, they had invited him to make them an offer. With his mind fixated on crest heights, he had thrown them a number just to placate them: it was blue-sky pricing, totally unrelated to any rational or logic. There wasn't even any discussion. Mocking his naivety, the Boston bankers had packed their boards, bags and Nespresso machine and flown back East. Two days later, after some cursory analysis and some tests on a spreadsheet, they had realised to their horror the extraordinary returns they could make with Kurt's simple code: his price was a steal.

Shuttling back to LA on the company's Lear jet, they rushed back to the beach and the Winnebago. For days they scoured the bars, cafes and waves. They were too late. Kurt had gone back to the mountains. They were in a Patagonia store buying extreme wet-weather gear when they were shocked to learn that he had settled with a rival – a rival, who only two years later (armed with Kurt's proprietary code), would go on to destroy them.

The young girl next to Kurt, Corran mistook to be his girlfriend. Cara, in her mid-twenties, was dressed as if she had just thrown all her pocket-money at a second-hand bazaar. With airy disregard for accepted style or fashion, she mixed hand-woven silks and traditional silver with garish lycra and Christmas-cracker diamante. She wasn't pretty, but her personality, impish, a touch scatty, was endearing. Andresen made light of her cheap 'hello kitty' iPhone case, a copy so shoddy it had already cracked and was now held together with tape. In turn, Cara ragged the billionaire over his faux 'street' style; a ripped rebel chic procured from the world's most exclusive stores. She could have bought his whole look from the local market at a fraction of the price and fed the population of Bhutan.

Corran warmed to Cara's trash ethnic aesthetic. Nothing was authentic, but, likewise, nothing was inauthentic. She bumped about in a bubble of her own making. Right or wrong, she cared little about propriety or convention. But just as Corran had been taken in by Kurt's nonchalant, beach-boy charm, he was to learn that Cara's junky, second-hand clothes and shallow banter, were, in her own sweet way, yet more deceptive.

Andresen had been introduced to Cara at SXSW, a media festival in Austin that mixed music, film and technology. They had shared a minibus with ten other festival goers booked to hear a new band at a remote art gallery on the outskirts of the city. Within ten minutes of light conversation (as casual as you can get in a mini bus rammed with obsessional coding geeks), he had realised that Cara was way too smart for college, even if that college was the much-lauded MIT. Barely in her second year and working evenings as a bar girl, she had laughed off his advances. But Andresen had been relentless in his pursuit. Eventually, turned by an offer she would have been crazy to refuse and sweetened by an Aladdin's cave of diamante and a truck load of Hershey bars, she was lured away. In Andresen's eyes, Cara was exceptional. Hers was the big bio-science breakthrough that would form the beating heart of his empire.

Cara's simple, powerful intuition was a radical advance that had transformed the reading of gene language. Rejecting established theory, Cara had treated genes like small beads, assembling the different components much as one would crochet a cushion cover. Her kitchen-sink insight added up to a much faster and more reliable method to conduct DNA synthesis. This was the key Andresen was looking for – speed and over-the-counter affordability. It would open the door to the design of foods that could be tailored to the needs of the world, rather than a coterie of multinationals. Individuals would once again be in control of their lives.

The extraordinary revelation that Cara was the true brains of the operation stunned Corran. Not that he should have been so wrong-footed by such obvious prejudices, that she was shockingly young and dressed like some dizzy back-up singer in a Nashville folk band. Anyone could have made the same mistake. The ruby stud through an eyebrow and a zombie tattoo on the back of her neck only added to the obfuscation. But to be all of those things and possess Einsteinesque powers of intellect, how could that be? Never before had he seen such a disconnect between outward appearance and mental ability. Surely someone with such exalted genius must in some way be psychologically impaired? Wasn't half of the geek meritocracy lorded over by princelings who were borderline autistic? But the longer he talked with Cara, the more he found such notions unfounded; she was sweet, sometimes flakey, capricious even, if not a touch flirtatious.

"I've read every one of your books," she said, "Tortured my parents by making a mess of one of your Tagine recipes. You're the reason I nearly flunked science at high school. And if I have to make a full, embarrassing disclosure, I even wrote you a grovelling letter to get a summer internship in your kitchen."

"Lucky for all of us then, that I threw it away," replied Corran.

Of course, he wouldn't have been able to remember, he received hundreds of applications from all over the world. Too many to answer. Yet in a surreal turnaround, just three years later, it appeared that their roles had reversed. When Andresen had been fishing to secure famous chefs for the project, it was Cara's insistence that had put Corran's name at the top of the list. In a way, he was only standing on a bamboo raft in the middle of the Mekong at half past one in the morning, because he had rejected her and she had accepted him.

Andresen, anxious to keep up the flow of introductions, moved Corran on through the room. Within Cara's team there were two programmers – John Chan and Howie Stockwell. In tech circles they were renowned for hitting the highest tier within the 10X elite, a talent pool for 'digital rockstars'. The ranking recognised the talent of software engineers whose output was ten times more effective than that of the average, and who came no doubt, with 10X salaries to boot.

Behind the tech team were the investors. Corran knew Carl Lindberg from New York. He had last seen him at his estate on Shelter Island. Corran was surprised how he had become part of Andresen's circus. And no small part at that. Andresen had quietly absorbed Font Lescari into his empire. Corran's modest property, *The Story of Food*, was thus already within the fold.

The biggest shock of the evening was seeing Jade again. The jolt was enough to break out sweat on his forehead. Like a dramatic still from a film noir, a fleeting shot of when he had last abandoned her at the Hiro San restaurant flashed up in his memory. The image made him wince with shame over how he had mistreated her. Not only had he callously used her connections to blag the precious table in the first place, he had pushed her through the embarrassing fiasco on the terrace. And then he had left Tokyo without a call; not even an email, text message, or emoji of explanation. Was she bitter, angry, had she forgotten? And then an added, niggling concern: What the hell was she doing here anyway? Surely she couldn't be part of Andresen's intimate circle?

Jade, looking immaculate as always, as if fresh from a photographer's studio, broke abruptly from the conversation she was having and reaching Corran, kissed him warmly on the cheek. She touched him in an affectionate way, much as one would stroke the velvet embroidery of a Prada jacket. It could mean one of only two things – that she had truly forgiven him, or, more unnervingly, masking her true emotions, was slowly hatching a plan of revenge.

"You never called me back?" she purred.

"I got caught. Had to swim from the pier. My mobile must have packed up in the water."

"Sounds unfortunate, Corran. You should take better care of yourself."

"Of course, you know each other," Andresen cut in.

Or did he? When Corran had first met Jade in Tokyo, her claim that she was a media entrepreneur was, he now realised, a simplification that verged on dishonesty. In reality she now ran her father's business empire. It had been an old-style commodity company – trucks, warehouses and ships. In the late eighties they had made fortunes when Communist China had opened its doors to commerce. But Jade, educated in the West, returned with more contemporary aspirations. She wasn't interested in docks, cranes and lego-like shipping containers. When her father passed away, she had banked the family fortune on transforming the old company into a powerhouse of the new. The warehouses along the sea-front in Shanghai were turned into a new tech centre, Quarto Shin. Emulating the start-up success of companies in the US, the company had rapidly cornered the market in search and online messaging. And when Andresen had looked to secure Asian partners, Quarto Shin was the obvious company of choice. Meeting with Jade and her brothers in New York, they had carved up continents of interest across the globe. A crude demarcation line had been drawn around the hemisphere. In effect, Jade was empress of the South.

The party continued. More introductions were made. Corran met job titles he didn't even know existed – innovation manager, chief growth hacker of marketing, global happiness officer. And still fresh faces passed by that he hadn't been introduced to. Was there another pier or boat from which they were streaming? Or was he just getting tired, forgetful or drunk?

It was late when, mercifully, the party began to wind down. Corran had taken to the beach to rest his legs, still aching after the bike ride over the hills. Reclining in the fine mica sand, he could look back across the water at those who still lingered. The investors had long gone. Kurt, feeling restless, had challenged some of the younger team members to kayak back to the hotel in Nong Khai, an eight-mile trip in pitch black with known sections of rapids. Cara's software geniuses and the younger creatives, had formed a semi-circle on the cushions. Spirits on the side table, they were playing mahjong.

Catching Andresen stifling a yawn, Corran felt gratified; the man wasn't immortal. Even a tech titan could run down.

Only a small, intimate circle remained standing at the corner of the pontoon – Favia, Jade and Amy. Looking like three scheming witches hatching a plan, they cut an icy silhouette against the shifting, glittering waters of the Mekong.

Favia, born into a family of Brazilian industrialists, was used to mixing with power and money. Jade, brought up a high-achieving tiger child, had leadership coursing through her veins. Only Amy was a novice. Her meteoric rise from back-packer drifter to executive boardroom had been extraordinary. Back home, her family siblings, two elder brothers and a sister who had never really left the safe confines of Auckland, would be astounded at her success.

Initially, pulled in by the force-field of Andresen's magnetism, Corran had rolled with the collective energy and optimism. Now in the shadows of the river bank, observing these people from afar, darker thoughts started to intrude. So this was his destiny? To be under the thumb of three beautiful but daunting women? To have his more wayward ideas, his ambitions and flights of fancy clipped by corporate doublespeak and buzzy mission statements? Maybe it was no more than he deserved, a fitting comeuppance for a history of ignoble transgressions.

Jade, he had certainly wronged. Judging by the quantity and passion of emails she had sent over the past, she had certainly been in love with him. Her close friends had castigated him for leading her on. But he had kept up the pretence and ruthlessly exploited her to unlock more doors and gain access to her influential friends. After accumulating so many favours and debts, her allegiance was highly unlikely...

He liked Favia. For someone so hopelessly wealthy, she was surprisingly self-effacing and conciliatory. Although given her relationship with Andresen and her anxiety to make her own mark, would those qualities hold true? A clash was surely inevitable.

What about Amy? Where would she stand? They were now equals. At least that's what it said on paper. But truly, at difficult impasses, when there were conflicts of opinion to be aired, would Amy, as part of the Favia and Jade triangle, still be on side? The fact that he had given her her first big break surely meant something. Of course, he had pushed her hard. She had worked long hours, never complained and never knowingly taken holidays. And because of it she had achieved a lot. But had he ever given her the credit she undoubtedly deserved, made her feel valued? Probably not. His thoughtless, crazed (in her eyes) behaviour over the past few days couldn't have helped.

Tiredness cut in. Lulled by the soft breeze and the lazy, ethereal music, he drifted in and out of sleep. Momentarily his eyelids closed. In a semi-dream state he had a fleeting vision of the three of them standing over a chopping block, long stainless steel knives in their hands, himself on the cold granite cutting surface, being finely sliced like so much *ceviche*.

Thirty One

A thick fog hung over the river. As the sun warmed, distant mountain peaks across the border in Laos lifted above the curtain of cloud. Fishermen, casting nets off the prows of thin wooden canoes, gradually emerged from the grey. Dropping from great heights, swifts flew in low over the glass-like surface, picking off water flies and bugs.

Despite the arduous night on the Mekong, Corran had got up early to see his silver-haired tour group depart. It was one of Amy's stipulations that he had sworn to observe. Not that he had felt coerced into making the move. He had grown to like the group. Of course one or two, having failed to forgive him for his failure to turn up over the first two days, had never thawed. Worse, they had read his anxiety to 'show some love' as a cynical panic-move designed to offset ill-feeling and the posting of bad reviews.

The rest had been surprisingly accepting of the gaping holes within their lavish schedule. It was true, his charm offensive had often ramped up into overdrive, but by doing so he had allowed himself to be more open, even displaying brief moments when his eccentricities veered into foolishness. The marked divide between 'celebrity' and 'paying guest' had become blurred. Corran went out of his way to expose them to experiences that ordinary travel groups might promise, but never have the nerve to deliver. Seeing the insides of a Lao border jail, replete with bamboo racks and torture pit, was certainly original. As was celebrating 'freedom' with Chinese Ningxia Nongken 'champagne'. Yes, at times they were irritatingly pedantic, over-opinionated and snappy (the impatience of old age and wealth), but they had also been refreshingly real, laughing at past foibles and disappointments.

Andresen's junglefest on the river had been a total contrast. Kurt, Cara, Howie and Chan; he had liked too. Who wouldn't? They were young, beautiful, funny, inspiring and articulate. And he had been seduced, awed, by their blend of energy, effortless brilliance and calm self-assurance. Theirs was a reading of the world, that devoid of barriers and obstacles, saw nothing but opportunity. It was as if they were playing out a computer game, in which landscapes were thick with prizes and rewards that just needed to be scooped up and banked along the smooth trajectory of their lives. This highway of fortune converged on a single visionary destination – Andresen's utopia. Here was a blueprint of noble halls, towers and glistening cathedrals. Corran too was on the inside. He was one of them, the elite, the chosen few. Yet, as he reflected on the undoubtedly impressive columns, squares and gilded domes of this brave new world, he felt only unease.

Andresen's flight crew, two young Austrian pilots and a meticulous Polish assistant, had arranged everything with quiet, unseen efficiency. Corran's bags had been picked up earlier from the hotel. A limousine had been arranged to take him, Amy and Kurt to the airport. They joined Andresen and Favia in an executive waiting room reserved for private jets. With their passports and paperwork handled behind the scenes, all they had to do was wait. A glass coffee-table was laid out with small pastries, sandwiches and cup-cakes. All were untouched. Everyone had been forewarned: Andresen's flight crew included Alice Yung, a Michelin-starred chef.

Two sides of the executive waiting room looked out over the tarmac. A line of dull-green military transport planes were parked up in the far distance. Worn canvas covers were roped around their cockpits and engine cowlings. Under their wings large pieces of their ailerons and tail sections lay scattered across the concrete. With grasses winding around their undercarriages, the planes looked so decrepit it was hard to believe they had ever flown.

In sharp contrast to the neglected military machines, Andresen's shiny, majestic Falcon 8X was being restocked and refuelled. A small group of airport personnel, having walked from the main terminal to examine the rare jet, had joined a circle of admirers around the nose cone of the plane to take pictures.

Andresen was a modest guy. He didn't make a big deal of his toys. Kurt, fast and loose with the numbers, had let slip the night before that a baseline version, without the bespoke interior and navigational extras, came in at a cool $58 million.

Corran took a seat on a large white leather sofa at the back of the lounge. Book shelves were stocked with a selection of international newspapers and obscure luxury magazines familiar only to those of 'high net worth'. A giant chandelier loomed over the modest space. Lending an air of seedy opulence to an otherwise soulless modern interior, the ornate glass arrangement looked like it had been lifted from the dining room of some failed African despot.

Small details betrayed neglect: a shrivelled lizard peered out from the grill of an air-conditioning unit; layers of dead flies collected in the opaque glass of an overhead skylight. On a marble plinth, a single orchid of unusually vivid colour, gathered dust.

With time on his hands, Corran's attention fell to his computer. Finding the wifi connection he checked through the international news. A coach-load of Catholic nuns had been kidnapped by militants in South Georgia. In New Mexico, a student had gunned down the lead singer in an a capella competition. And in the business news, the international bond market was heading for a precipitous meltdown.

Dispirited by the world view, Corran clicked out of the news feed. Windows from previous web pages and searches filled the screen; entries from Wiki, a book purchase from Amazon, reference sources on Thai spices and herbs. He hit the 'close' icons and one by one, like a stack of cards collapsing, the pages disappeared. One last window remained. It showed a satellite image of the countryside around

Chaiyaphum. He had last used Google maps before driving out on his fruitless search with Dao, the deceitful deputy manager. Within the image he could make out the vague outline of the restaurant and the lake. Grainy and blurred, the picture wasn't as sharp as he remembered. It was as if the clarity of the image had faded and deteriorated over time (although knowing that digital files never degrade he was faintly aware how goofy that sounded). What secrets and mysteries the place might have hidden were now further veiled in dark, impenetrable pixels and muddy tones. As Corran mulled over this last image, he allowed himself to reflect on his painful failure, a distressing chapter that was now, mercifully closed.

Kurt, having broken from a conversation around the main window, joined Corran on the sofa. Pathologically nosey when it came to any screen – iPhone, iPad, iWatch, he craned his neck over Corran's shoulder to peer at his outdated machine.

"That map browser is useless," Kurt interjected.

"You have a better one?" asked Corran.

"Of course," the words bursting forth so predictably.

Kurt didn't do 'off the shelf' retail. Everything in his lifestyle orbit, from his Italian tailored shirts and Mykita shades to his Bianchi carbon composite bike, was bespoke. His Apple laptop was no exception. Given to him personally by Jonathan Ive's inner design team, the ARX3 was still some years from the open market. Appearing to possess some inner sixth sense, it started instantly before Kurt had even picked it out of his rucksack. Flipping open the screen, he passed the pristine machine across to Corran.

"It uses voice recognition and AI. Read off the co-ordinates from your previous search. Then you can make an accurate comparison," Kurt suggested as he got up from the sofa.

"Take your time. I need some coffee."

Initially Corran found it frustrating getting used to Kurt's future thinking technology. It didn't even have a keyboard, yet the browser window opened without being instructed. Remembering Kurt's guidance to dictate the coordinates, within micro-seconds of him speaking, the results had appeared. Naturally, he had expected Kurt's machine to be superior in every way – better screen, faster processor, more pixels, higher resolution – but he wasn't prepared for the leap in clarity that occurred when the image of the restaurant and the lake came up on screen. Whereas the picture on his own feeble machine looked like it had been viewed through several layers of thick, dirty smog, Kurt's screen had the unnerving detail of a photograph taken from a drone in bright sunlight. More than seeing the shapeless blobs of chairs and tables, he could make out the details of the tired paper lanterns hung across the bushes, the bedraggled plants on the veranda, even the outlines of two further cars submerged in the dark murky waters of the lagoon. But it wasn't the exceptional definition that shocked Corran the most. The new image revealed an entirely new perspective to the site that had previously been hidden, details he hadn't noticed before.

Behind the small shack on stilts, steps led over a bridge to the far bank. From the muddy shore, a well-worn path wound its way through long grasses up a hill to the edge of a forest. And within a clearing, half-shadowed by a dark circle of trees, stood a second building. A dense column of smoke could be seen rising from an opening in its roof. It revealed the presence of a kitchen.

Thirty Two

Corran hit the brakes hard. He would have hit the small child if his primal instincts hadn't cut through the dull fog of his confusion and fired up the motor neurons necessary to stamp his foot to the floor. The tyres screamed, a puff of smoke lifted, black rubber marked the tarmac. The young girl, dancing in a bright orange butterfly dress with her back to the car, floated down the road oblivious to the danger. She didn't even turn around. Her mother, with a clearer view of the junction, saw it all. She pushed her way through the crowd and, grabbing her daughter, pulled her sharply to the side. Wrapping her arm protectively around the girl's shoulder, she led her away, casting an angry glance at the dumb foreigner in the hire car now stalled in the traffic.

A festival was taking place on the outskirts of town. Schoolchildren in multi-coloured dresses wore silver ornaments and flowers in their hair. Paper masks of wild animals and birds were carried on bamboo poles. A large cheering crowd, having spilled out of the offices and shops onto the main highstreet, gathered behind a group of musicians playing drums. Passersby on the sidewalk, both locals and travellers, hurrying to catch up with the procession, wrapped around both sides of Corran's now immobile car. Impatient as he was to get out of town, he could only sit it out and wait. Through the windscreen he could see a group of excited American tourists rushing to the scene. Hearing the echo of the drums, they were anxious not to miss out on recording the dancers. One at the front, an aspiring professional with several expensive Nikons strapped to his neck, had sprinted to the head of the procession and, lying in the road, raced through his aperture settings in a frenzied attempt to capture the vibrancy and colour of the moment. He was a large man and his belly, pulling from his undersized T-shirt, folded over the worn and dirty tarmac. With his finger pressed hard to the shutter release, he didn't seem to mind.

Corran could imagine the image filling the centre-pages of a travel magazine or the pristine white walls of an out-of-town art gallery – a moody micro-second snapshot of light and dark, bodies and limbs locked at odd angles, expressive faces starring out, their mouths and lips twisted in unnatural ways.

On his cooking titles over the years Corran had worked with a number of respected photographers. Anxious to distance himself from the sterility of studio pack-shots, he had turned to photojournalists to add an edge of realism and grit to his more exotic recipes. More at home in the jungles of Borneo or the mountains of Turkestan, they were hard drinkers and spurned the fussiness of stylists or art directors. Loyal to battered, war-scuffed 35mm cameras, these auteurs placed an almost obsessive importance on the raw objectivity of such frozen moments to capture truth. But wasn't stamping veracity on singular slices of time in itself a distortion? Taking in the crowd outside – the young, the middle-aged, the old, the infirm – every face possessed its own timeline of images. Intricate narratives of where they had come from and where they would go to; rich destinies that would play out in an infinite tapestry of possible actions, outcomes, dreams, aspirations and disappointments; tales that would pass by untold.

Fireworks went off at the edge of the canal. Looking over the heads of the dancers, Corran caught a glimpse of a light burning fiercely above the tree-line, climbing rapidly into the sky. Dazzlingly white, with wings like an angel, it soared in a powerful trajectory as if it would never come down. Corran waited for the shower burst to come when it reached its zenith. But it wasn't a firework – it was a plane

– Andresen's Falcon. He remembered that there were eight windows along the cigar-shaped fuselage. One was now empty.

Was this Corran's own snapshot? His future that might have been, the destiny he had rejected, now disappearing into the heavens? How many yet-to-be realised futures and horizons was he turning his back on? Bigger, better, more successful versions of himself, entities that were right now being erased from the pages of the great book of beings that were yet to be written?

From such a height, Corran was certain that they could see the procession below them. Was Amy at that same moment at one of those windows looking down? Was she furiously scratching out his name from one of her numerous spreadsheets, even now over-writing his entry with a second, better, more salubrious replacement? Maybe she had already done that homework. Maybe that list of 'alternatives' already existed.

The jet banked hard to the left. It made the direction-change with a balletic flourish, as if Andresen himself was in the cockpit, instructing his pilots to gesture a final, ostentatious 'fuck off' in the sky.

This last image of the plane, a distant white v-sign in a clear, cerulean sky, stayed in his mind a long time as he drove. With no fixed idea of which route he was taking, without guidance from road signs or street maps, Corran continued with a single warped directive dictating his moves.

Thirty Three

On the outskirts of Udon, the towering logos of the out-of-town supermarket chains, Big C, Tesco Lotus, even a pick-up truck ablaze in the car park at Homeland, passed without registering in Corran's fevered thoughts. Breaking from the town, the messy urban sprawl gave way to flat open countryside.

The Isarn region, notoriously arid, hadn't seen rain for more than nine months. Barren fields, emaciated trees, rough reed shelters and a family of sleeping buffalo; all were dusted in the same oppressive ochre hue. In one clearing, the emaciated husk of a Chinook helicopter lay scattered across the terrain, its shell now shelter for goats from the blazing heat.

The authorities had planned to build a reservoir. Politicians came from the city. Speeches were made, surveys undertaken and plans drawn up. But a minor dispute between warring interest groups, rice farmers and local industrialists, embroiled them in a bitter battle over water rights. Minor government officials were busy behind the scenes siphoning off the investment. By the time a painful settlement was reached, the hoped-for funds had long disappeared, leaving both sides with a mountain of debts, no result and no water.

The conflict left a bitter legacy. For mile upon mile the excavations remained, banked earth foundations and dusty empty squares, littered with rusting caterpillar trucks and abandoned diggers.

The featureless landscape mirrored Corran's own tired physiognomy. With hope of a petrol station or coffee shop evaporating with every monotonous turn, the empty expanse roused his hunger and thirst. He remembered that he hadn't eaten since morning. Anticipating the meal on the plane, he had missed breakfast.

At the airport, Amy, probably the only one not suffering from a cataclysmic hangover, had offered to find some fresh coffee. Naturally, the expensive coffee machine in the private terminal wasn't working. She had walked to the main terminal. It was further than she thought. By the time she had returned with some much needed espressos, Corran had already disappeared. Kurt's computer was still lying open on the now-empty seat. Her heart sank when she glanced at the screen. Immediately guessing its import, she had run to the carpark only to see a small silver hatchback speed out of the airport gates. She screamed out, but her voice, drowned by the roar of a departing 737, wasn't heard. For seconds she was at a loss as to what to do. She reached for her mobile and searched through her call history.

Thirty Four

Dao was fast asleep in the back-room office when he got the call from Amy. He hadn't slept well the night before. He had woken at uneven hours with a nagging unease, a premonition that despite the success of his endeavours a few days before, he somehow wasn't entirely free of the irritating, troublesome Australian. Amy's call confirmed that dread. His only faint consolation was that thanks to his night-time turmoil, his mind had already played through every possible permutation and course of action. He awoke clear as to what needed to be done.

By the time Dao had arrived at the lay-by near the lake, his associates, Chin, the police chief and Bao, the district officer, were already there puffing through a packet of Marlboro cigarettes. Music was playing from Chin's car. It was a familiar tune. In fact, it was the karaoke they had sung along to on the evening when they had first met the foreigner. Chin liked to refer to it as 'their song'. As Dao approached, he could see the police captain stamping the dust with his heel to the hard bass beat of the chorus. As there was already a sizeable dent in the dried red earth at his side, he must have been there some time. Bao, joining in with this impromptu band, rapped the hood of his pick-up truck with the flat of his hand.

Dao hated the song. Every chord, every set of notes were like beads of molten metal dripping into the inner recesses of his being, rekindling his guilt and remorse. When Dao was at his lowest ebb, often late at night drinking alone, a single note was enough to set off the entire dreaded melody.

Chin was well aware of the effect of the music. He had used the song, not to celebrate some shared memory, but as something grimly divisive – a morbid anthem to cement an ugly partnership forged in the past. A partnership of secrets and silence woven together in the place they were right now about to revisit.

It was a long time back, more than six years. Dao had just relocated to the area after the unfortunate incident in Bangkok. He had got to know Chin in his first months in his new job as manager at the Namsai Golden Resort, having called in the police after an incident over a forged credit card.

Chin was a young cadet when he had first been sent to Isarn. Never a popular posting for new recruits, the district was a poor province with little opportunity for advancement or financial reward from fines and bribes. Because of these lean returns, job turnover was high. It wasn't long before Chin had been offered promotion. Bao, three years into his job as deputy councillor, had headed the appointment committee.

Dao, anxious to ingratiate himself with his new circle of friends, had organised a celebration for Chin's promotion, an opportunity to show largesse Bangkok style. It turned into a big affair. He wanted to make a memorable impression.

As well as Chin, Bao and their immediate friends and family, local government officials and the owners of several businesses had been invited. Although Black Pig, a heavy metal band from Khon Kaen, had failed to turn up, Dao had managed to rig up his home stereo and a borrowed karaoke machine to the sound system. A drinks' importer who worked for the hotel, had agreed to supply beer and whisky at close to trade price.

With rumours of so much free drink on tap, the guest list had expanded. Staff had been a problem. The two young and relatively inexperienced waitresses at the lake restaurant couldn't cope. Chin had supplemented the team with four bar girls he knew from a nightclub in town.

For Dao, still used to Bangkok etiquette, perhaps the place cards had been a mistake. For those whose only interest was eating and drinking as much as they could in the shortest possible time, the formality of table plans had brought nothing but an embarrassed silence. When the first guests had finished gorging themselves and started sneaking back to their cars and pick-ups, Dao appeared anxious that his extravaganza was unravelling. It took Chin, grabbing a tray of free spirits, to stoke up the necessary fun and vitality.

The tables were cleared, the music stepped up and the dancing and karaoke began. The girls from the nightclub, glad to be liberated from their tedious waitressing duties, discarded their unflattering aprons and took to the stage. Dancing in short sequin skirts and cropped lycra tops, they were quickly the centre of attention.

Half-way through the second song, the dancing girls were coaxed down from the platform to circle the tables and guests. Chin, Dao and Bao needed little encouragement to join in. Draining their glasses and pushing back from their table, they were soon on their feet, stamping their Buckaroo-style cowboy boots and drunkenly shouting out in the wake of the four dancers. Chin, fuelled with beer and Thai whisky, made a dangerous and bullish clown. Romping about the veranda and swaying to the music, he reached out in vain attempts to grope the lithe singers.

The local girls watched nervously from the shadows. They weren't so chaste not to know where events were heading. Village celebrations – a birth, a marriage, a divorce – often played out in similar style. With free spirits and cheap drugs (*yaba*, known as 'crazy medicine'), a thin divide separated a benign fun-loving smile from a malevolent sneer, innocent tomfoolery from acts of mindless brutality.

And the youngest of these girls had good reason to keep a discreet distance. With a natural beauty and grace that effortlessly outshone the heavily-painted faces of the older bar girls, she had already attracted unwanted attention from the men. Attempting to distance herself from the horseplay and look busy, she had taken it upon herself to clear the remaining plates and dishes from the tables, a task that had since multiplied now that the bar girls had abandoned their waitressing for the dance floor. But her obvious discomfort with the party only made her more conspicuous, marking her out as a target for the leery behaviour of the crowd.

"So sad, so serious," "Why so uptight, like a nun, chill out, have fun," went the calls, "Sit, sit, join us, come closer, have a drink…"

As the village girl turned once again for the safety of the kitchen, arms stacked with dishes and cutlery, she collided with the twisting crocodile line of revellers steaming round the corner of the veranda. Chin happened to be at the front, maybe he had timed it that way. Her hip hit against his side, the cold handle of his gun protruding from his gunbelt. He was so close she could smell the crude whisky on his breath and see that he hadn't shaved that morning. Chin pretended he was startled, as if he hadn't noticed her before. Still acting the goat, he made out he was fainting, shading his eyes as though overcome by her brilliance. The girl, not knowing how to respond, nor even wanting to, froze. Taking advantage of her confusion, he leant forward and attempted a clumsy kiss. She reeled back. The plates in her arms unbalanced and crashed to the floor. For seconds there was silence. Then from all sides came the sound of loud, raucous, mocking laughter. Some threw their paper cocktail umbrellas at her.

Chin, seeing her distress, turned to quell the cruel crowd, his arms held aloft like a referee at one of his son's boxing matches. He made a big play of consoling her, softly putting a protective arm around her shoulder, whilst his other hand strayed between her legs. Close to tears, she pulled away screaming. Dao sensing the tension, attempted to intervene. But Chin was too far gone to be tamed. With all eyes in the crowd now focused on the developing drama, Dao's weak caution only made Chin more showy and belligerent. Getting theatrical, he made light of the girl's hysteria by aping her voice. "Eeeii, Eeeiii", he squealed. His girly antics softened his grip on her arm. Able to break away, she started running across the small bridge. He caught up with her and grabbing her wrist, hauled her back. She turned, suddenly fierce, her hand flying out and slapping him hard in the face.

Chin's precious aviator glasses flew off, hitting the floor. The buffoonery stopped. He let her go. Calmly bending down to the ground, he scrambled around the base of a table and eventually found his precious shades. Slowly he seated himself and reaching for a silk cloth from his side pocket, anxiously started polishing the scuffed lenses. It had little effect. They were cracked.

"The glass is cracked," he muttered.

"I'll get you another pair in Bangkok." Dao quickly interjected, joining him at the table and distracting him with a newly-opened bottle of vodka, "I'm going there anyway on business..."

"That's not the point," growled Chin, "She broke them. She's bad. Very bad. She needs to be punished."

"Why waste time with some stupid peasant girl?" replied Dao. He pointed to the dancing girls on the stage, "There are plenty of others... with bigger tits too."

"She needs to be punished," Chin repeated, still pointlessly polishing the broken lenses. His head nodded cryptically in the direction of the wooden shack. Bao, already holding the crying girl in a vice-like grip, needed little encouragement. He started dragging her across the veranda towards the kitchen. Wolf whistles and cheers, echoing from the tables, egged him on. As they crossed the small bridge, the girl's legs kicked out, frantically attempting to latch onto the bannister rail to prevent herself being dragged away. Her flip-flop came off and fell from the walkway into the water.

"Grab her legs, Dao!" barked Chin, rising from the table.

Dao, sheepishly following, reluctantly complied.

At the kitchen block, Bao kicked open the kitchen door. They dragged the writhing girl inside. Chin followed. The door was closed. The interior, dim and gloomy, was empty. With one arm, Chin swept the table clear of plates and glasses. Bao threw the girl to the surface, holding her down by her shoulders.

"Dao, take her other arm."

Dao did it. But he was nervous. He'd never done this type of thing before – beat a girl – if that really was their aim. But glancing across at the brutal actions of his two companions, now pressing the shrieking, defenceless girl to the table, he quickly began to revise his thinking; he knew what Chin's punishment would entail, what would happen. He was unsure of himself and how he should react. Was this a test? Some bullish initiation ceremony to show he was tough enough to be in their gang? Was he going to have to take part, take her too? As he looked down at the helpless girl twisting on the table top, this was his greatest fear. Not that he didn't like sex. He had been with many girls in several clubs and bars. Who hadn't? But this was different. It was against her will. It was rape. Of course he shouldn't be doing it, it was wrong, against the law. But what was the law? This was the law. Chin, the police chief, spreading a girl's legs apart and tearing at the buckle on his trousers; Bao, the district officer, greedy eyes shining in the half-light, pouring vodka over her breasts.

Dao, consumed by anxiety and doubt, momentarily weakened. Sensing his grip relax, the girl was able to tear her arm away. Kicking and screaming, her hand lashed out. Her fingers caught Chin, nails tearing into the side of his face.

"Hold her down you idiot!" snapped Chin, pulling back from her flailing claws. Dao managed to grab the loose arm and wrestle it back to the table. Having fought free once, she was harder to subdue. He found he needed to apply all his strength to keep her from breaking away a second time. How someone so young, so thin, could fight back against the three of them amazed him. And even though he was one of those men struggling to subdue her, he found himself perversely admiring her spirit and courage. Aggression warped into empathy; he wanted to lean forward, hold her and lick the tears from her eyes; he wasn't like them, he was on her side, wanted to care and look after her. For some reason he found himself softly caressing her cheek in some deranged belief he was comforting her. But his vain attempts to sooth her only made her wriggle more and howl louder – he had no idea why. Panicked by her yelling, he pressed his hand tightly over her mouth to muffle her screams. Breaking away, she caught the side of his hand fumbling over her mouth and bit hard. The searing, unbelievable pain shot through the nerves of his arm. Her young teeth had gone deep. Blood poured from his lacerated thumb.

"You stupid fucking bitch!" he bellowed. Couldn't she understand he was trying to console her, trying to help?

Dao snatched the whisky bottle from Bao, took a deep swig and sprayed it all over her face. Glaring into his eyes with a look of intense venom, the girl spat back, hitting him directly in the eye. Dao, enraged, grabbed the nearest object at hand, a stone mortar, and swinging it in a brutal arc above his head, brought it down across the side of her face. There was a horrible dull thud. With a grim sense of foreboding he realised he had hit her hard – too hard.

"She bit me," he bleated pathetically, sucking the blood dripping from his thumb.

Thirty Five

Bao went to the head of the table. Taking the girl's shoulders, he attempted to shake her back to consciousness. She didn't respond.

Dao, standing back in the shadows, was perplexed. Why didn't she move? He had only hit her once. It wasn't that hard. She must be pretending. If she was, she had better snap out of it. Didn't she realise it would only make them more angry?

Chin, looking down at the lifeless form below him, broke the silence, "What the fuck, Dao? What the fuck was that all about?"

"She's just messing with us", muttered Dao, nervously.

Summoning up some dying bravado, he stepped forward again. He leant over the table and slapped her face. There was no reaction. A second time he hit her harder. Still nothing. He would have hit her a third and fourth time, if Bao hadn't intervened and pulled him away.

"It's no good, Dao," muttered Bao, "Back off."

"What do you mean it's no good? She's just pretending, she'll come round, she'll..."

"I don't think so," cut in Chin, tucking his shirt back into his trousers and adjusting the buckle on his belt.

For several seconds no more was said. In the icy stillness the music from outside intruded. Loud and raucous, it was Chin's familiar tune, the crass chorus, "It's my money, money", coming at them from all angles through the paper-thin walls.

Dao stood there stupefied, rooted to the spot. Panicked, his mind raced for an escape, a solution, a plan, some ray of hope that might negate, deny the inevitable, horrific reality lying still on the table in front of him: Why the fuck didn't she move?

"Get a bag," was Chin's only bleak response.

"Why?" pleaded Dao, shocked by the suggestion and all that it entailed.

"What if she's still alive? Shouldn't we call for help? Find a doctor? Your pick-up, Bao. Your pick-up can get her to hospital."

"After what's happened here, you'd have to be out of your mind!" snapped Chin.

They pushed Dao aside. A rough hessian sack was found at the back of a cupboard. Chin and Bao lifted the girl's body into the bag. Together they dragged the lifeless form to the back of the hut.

"Dao, go to the front, check no one's around," hissed Bao.

Numb with terror, he took time to respond.

"Dao, check the fucking door!" Chin shouted.

Eyes dead, like a man condemned, Dao staggered across the short space to the entrance. Cautiously he pulled back the edge of the door and peered outside. Although the party continued as before, he saw no lights, no people, tables or chairs – just terror. Terror, that standing just outside, swirled like a pestilent cloud of wanton malevolence, its tentacles reaching out and swarming through every pore of his body.

At the far end of the shack, Chin opened the back door. A thin wooden ledge overlooked the back of the lake. Together with Bao he lifted the girl outside. She wasn't heavy, but the sacking, worn and torn in places, split apart. Bao found some string. They tied it around the base of the sack, but the twine, old and brittle, broke easily. Bao had to wrap it several times around the body to keep it taut.

Chin stepped down to the water's edge. Reaching into the shallows he found some rocks. Together they filled the sack with enough stones to weigh it down. Winding a thick electrical cable around the neck of the bag, Bao dragged the sack to the edge of the ledge. With Chin supporting the weight of the body, Bao pushed the bag over the ledge and let it roll over the side into the water. Chin, gradually releasing his grip, let it drop into the gloom.

The body sank quickly and silently into the muddy dark waters. Squatting on the edge of the ledge, they waited several minutes just to be sure. Small bubbles lifted from the depths. The sudden splash of a large catfish erupting from the surface spooked them, making Bao jump back from the shore. Then the waters went still. The dull, impenetrable ripples were replaced by the still reflection of low clouds, silhouetted by moonlight.

Putting the girl into the water so close to the shack wasn't the best plan. The two were well aware that their hiding place was only temporary, their intention being to return in the morning when they had more time, retrieve the body and dispose of the evidence properly.

Chin and Bao returned to the party. They made up a convincing story. After Chin had punished the girl for slapping him, beating her with his belt, she had run crying back to her village. Dao had chased after her to bring her back; there were still dishes, glasses and pans to wash. That was fifteen minutes ago. The fool, too much of a city boy, must have got lost.

No one had any reason not to believe their tale. One or two even clapped. Stupid girl – what on earth had possessed her to slap a police officer – she obviously deserved it.

The following day the three returned. Chin had brought spades, long wooden poles and a roll of heavy-duty nylon chord. No one was at the restaurant. They thought it would be easy. But despite a hot laborious afternoon probing and digging through the sticky silt, the body of the girl couldn't be found. Although this failure only revived Dao's fears, Chin read this minor setback as an advantage. Maybe they hadn't done such a bad job after all. The heavy rocks he and Bao had added to the sack must have dragged her down into the soft sediment.

The lake was deep. If they couldn't find her, no one could. The task was effectively done. If no one talked, they were safe.

After a month, and at Dao's request, they had met up a long way from Chaiyaphum at a service station on the main highway to Khon Kaen. Dao, pale and worn, didn't look great. Plagued by guilt and remorse, he had been beset with afflictions – anxiety fits, an erratic heartbeat, constant headaches. Chin, laughing at his childish frailties, told him he was just being over-sensitive. The remedy was simple.

"Get out, get drunk, fuck girls."

Such distractions would ensure that his silly concerns would gradually fade away; just as she would fade away, he mischievously added; the maggots will have gotten to her body and eaten it away. The important thing, the only important thing, was to keep away from the place, be normal.

But Dao couldn't keep away or be normal. The restaurant, abandoned after the incident, closed down. Late at night he would return to the veranda overlooking the lake and peer down into the inky, grim waters, searching for some sign, some clue that she wasn't really there, that none of this had happened.

He still remembered her face. That innocence, that beauty, those powerful mesmerising eyes still haunted and tormented him. At night, he didn't have the courage to sleep in the dark. He kept the overhead lights on and tuned his television to MTV so that music videos played relentlessly at full volume in the background.

Often, in those rare moments that he did find sleep, he dreamed about her. He fantasised that she was a singer and he was her lover, come to save her and take her to a better place, a home in a townhouse, three floors and a roof terrace with a view to a beach.

Day and night Dao yearned for her, real or unreal, angel or ghost, as if his desperate, belated affection might buy some redemption.

Thirty Six

The fuel warning light had been flickering on the dashboard of the small hatchback for at least half an hour. Corran hadn't noticed it. The warning was lost within an array of secondary flashing lights; bulb failure, low oil pressure and larger LED text: 'urgent service required'.

For the past ten miles his progress had been painfully slow. The road looked like it hadn't been repaired for years. Large potholes, which occasionally stretched the entire width of the tarmac, pitted the highway like the surface of Mars. Steering a path through this obstacle course had been difficult. Once or twice he had misjudged his line and a front tyre had slammed into a deep hollow with enough force to shred the rubber from the rim.

Beyond distant hills, an ominous line of dark cloud looked like it had been etched onto the sky with a black marker pen, too comical to be real. He wasn't unduly concerned; on all sides there was nothing but clear skies and sunshine. In some ways he welcomed shade as stupidly he had left his sunglasses behind on the sofa in the luxury airport lounge.

What Corran couldn't sense, comfortably cocooned in his air-conditioned, sound-insulated cabin, was the sharp drop in temperature and the dramatic shift in wind direction. Large thunderstorms are common in Southeast Asia. Forming over the Northwestern Pacific, they sweep in across the seas, gathering momentum over the high mountain ranges of Vietnam and Laos, before dropping to the flatter plains of Thailand. Drawing in warm moist air as fuel, they create areas of low pressure, which in turn, much like a Dyson vacuum cleaner, sucks in cooler air from the surroundings. With wind speeds that can get beyond two hundred kilometres an hour, a cluster of towering cumulonimbus, capped by their distinctive anvil-shaped crown, can quickly become perilous.

When drops of water first dotted the windscreen, Corran thought he had just ploughed into a cloud of unfortunate bugs. Deceptively, it was still oppressively bright overhead. But the transition from a state of innocent blue skies to dark shadow was inexplicably violent. It was like driving into a wall of water so dense it was as if he had hit a physical barrier. Visibility that had previously stretched to far horizons was abruptly cut to yards. The wind roared across the barren landscape in powerful, cyclical bursts. Driven by the gale, raindrops hammered like ball-bearings onto the bonnet, roof and sides of the car. Under the pressure of a near constant cascade, the weak wiperblades struggled to maintain their rhythm. The camber of the road surface, too flat to drain the weight of water became impenetrable. Weaving the car between these deep pools caused the hatchback to rock alarming from left to right, setting off an erratic cadence aggravated by gusts punching in from the sides.

At certain points Corran peered over the crest of a hill to see nothing but a lake-like expanse in front of him, the tips of small bushes and fence posts his only clue as to the edge of the road. In a lay-by ahead, a line of pick-up trucks and buses had wisely pulled over. Its occupants, pressing their faces to the fogged-up glass, watched as Corran's car foolishly persevered.

A mile further on, a ten-wheeled truck hadn't been so lucky. Its driver, having misjudged a corner, had slid off the road and rolled into a canal. Bags of spilled cement, mixing with mud on the grass verges, formed into sticky, cloudy pools.

At a further intersection, the water surging over a crossroads was so deep as to break over the bonnet. For seconds the struggling hire car went limp in his hands – a rudder would have been more use than a steering wheel.

Impossibly the weight of rain across the windscreen intensified. As the visibility further deteriorated, Corran was filled with a deepening unease, a sense of foreboding that what he was encountering was more than just freak weather. The brutality of the howling wind and rain felt like a metaphysical force, an unnatural presence, its giant arms and legs actively pushing him back.

Corran drove on, his frame bent over the steering wheel, struggling to decipher the road. Unknowingly, he had long passed Chaiyaphum. No landmarks, turnings or signs registered in his vision. It was only by chance that he caught the remains of the distinctive billboard of the beer girl in the red bikini swinging overhead. The violence of the storm had torn more than half of the image away. Only the lower section of the hoarding, depicting her lithe legs and the struggling half-crocodile men, remained.

Realising he was coming in too fast to make the turn, Corran hit the brakes. The car, sliding on the uneven tarmac, momentarily broke out of line. It hit the far bank and collided with the remains of the top half of the billboard, the girl's bright, effervescent grin filling his side window. Shaken but unhurt, Corran snapped the shift into reverse, swung the car around and continued.

The narrow country lane was no easier to navigate – branches, torn bushes and dead banana leaves obscured the surface. Corran soon arrived at the familiar crossing and took the track to the left. As the road wound down to the valley, he knew that the bridge over the river would be his last big challenge.

Reaching the bottom of the hill, he stopped. So swollen was the river that the banks on both sides were barely visible. Most of the length of the bridge was submerged in a shifting, ugly brown current. The tame warning signs, set up to deter him three days before, had long since been swept away, torn tapes on the posts the only evidence that they had ever been there.

Despite the added risk, Corran locked his eyes on the exit posts at the far end of the bridge, hit the accelerator and propelled the small Honda mercilessly into the current.

Mid-way across the divide the water was at its most turbulent. As the wheels rolled over the mid-section of the bridge, a rotten plank came loose and shattered. The right side of the hatchback broke through the gaping cavity. The river surged. A violent crest shot up against the side windows, ramming the car against the flimsy side barrier. The engine howled as momentarily the wheels lost traction. Only the car's momentum was enough to prevent it from being rolled over the side into the churning waves.

With steam pouring from a shattered exhaust, the battered Honda made it to the far bank. Sliding in the deep mud at the base of the bridge, Corran coaxed the struggling machine up the steep incline. Half-way up the hill, the car veered abruptly against rocks at the edge of the track. Corran stamped the accelerator. There was an unearthly shudder from underneath, as if something large and rubbery had wrapped itself around the half-shaft. The front wheels screamed, smoke poured from the rim, before the tread eventually found grip and jumped free from the gully. Although Corran managed to bring the car back to the centre of the road, several deep gashes had been torn in the sidewall of the front tyre. Despite this, the hatchback limped on, struggling to make it the last thousand metres to the parking space in the now-familiar grass bank. As Corran turned into the space, the shredded tyre, finally pulling itself from the hub, collapsed. Seconds later the engine, starved of fuel, gave out.

Thirty Seven

Corran removed the key from the ignition. The windscreen wipers came to rest, marring the glass with a last opaque streak of raw umber. The rain stopped. There was silence. Eerily mimicking his first visit, powerful shafts of sunlight punched though the damp foliage and illuminated the previously hostile surroundings. But this time he wasn't alone. Only yards in front, he could see a line of cars: Dao's distinctive Isuzu, Bao's pick-up and Chin's sinister black Mercedes. He was troubled. Why were they here, what were they doing?

Corran got out of his battered car. Around him, steam rose up from the damp earth and bushes. Raindrops dripping from overhead branches rolled down his neck and back. He passed the parked cars and peered in through the side windows. In Chin's Mercedes a half-finished cup of Starbucks coffee sat lukewarm in the cup-holder. He had obviously not planned to stay long; carelessly he had even left his gun belt and a two-way radio on the passenger seat. In Bao's pick up, a thick green tarpaulin covered the flat-bed. A corner of the cover had been untied and pulled aside. Beneath it he could see the outline of several large petrol canisters.

It was remarkably still. There was no movement in the trees or sound from the surroundings. Although he couldn't sense that anyone was around, he called out cautiously, "Hello, hello," as if he were a lost postman delivering mail or a gas bill to a remote address. There was no answer.

Taking the track through the long grass, Corran climbed the steps to the platform. He found the veranda in disarray. Several tables and chairs had been broken up and piled in an untidy stack. Three petrol containers stood nearby. Two were empty. Dark black marks scarred the floorboards, as if the three had attempted to set alight to the pyre of smashed furniture, but failed. At the centre of this pile a faint glow still emanated from weak embers within the ashes. Harder to explain was a spray of blood on the floorboards – and at the end of the mark, more cryptically, a shattered lens. It was from Chin's much coveted sunglasses.

A dog barking beyond the trees made Corran glance up. Beyond the rusty roof of the kitchen block, mid-way up a hill overlooking the plain, a curl of smoke climbed into the sky.

Despite the returning humidity, Corran felt strangely cold, ill at ease. That sense of trepidation and dread that had crept over him imperceptibly throughout the drive in the storm, had now coalesced into a discomforting numbing weight inside, draining him of will and energy.

Seeing the broken chairs, the botched fire, the blood and broken lenses, Corran didn't need to be much of a detective to work out that what had happened, or indeed, what was still happening, didn't augur well. Every rational, prudent, cautious cell in his body, shrieked "Leave! Run! Get back to the safety of the hire car and never come back!" Even before this chorus of internal complaint had formed into a conscious directive he had already made a retreat to the exit. Indeed, Corran was close to the base of the steps and the track back to the car, when an equally forceful impulse arrested him mid-step.

Something passed in the wind, something alluring, enticing – a distant scent. Initially it was so slight and fleeting, he passed it off as no more than a mild aberration brought on by his own deep hunger. But then a second, more powerful trace was carried by the breeze and captured by his senses. This time the aromas were more distinct. As his mind honed in on its imprint, an image clearer than a photograph fused in his consciousness. In exacting, almost microscopic detail, he saw the dish from the fateful evening, so distinct in his memory that he could read the blades of the coriander leaves and the fine shreds of kaffir. Beguiled by the stark clarity of this vision, all the fear and indecision that had previously corroded his purpose, melted away. New imperatives came to the fore. It was clear that the smells were coming from the top of the hill. It was from within the circle of trees he had seen so clearly on Kurt's map. He had to know what and who was there.

Crossing the small bridge, Corran found a track through bushes that wound around the back of the shack. A narrow pathway led through marshland thick with bullrushes and wild sugarcane skirting the edge of the lake. Old railway sleepers had been embedded in the sticky sediment. On both sides, stagnant putrid water oozed with rotting plant life.

On the far side of the marsh, Corran discovered the sandy track that snaked through the low bushes up the hill. Kurt's impressively detailed satellite image had shown a distinctive 'S'-shaped path climbing up through the valley to the circle of trees at the top of the rise. But the 'bird's eye' view had failed to take into account the depth of vegetation. Feather reed grass, its wispy seed heads bent and broken by the violence of the storm, blurred the contours of the track, making it difficult for Corran to orientate himself within the undergrowth.

Up ahead, chillingly silhouetted against a falling sun and framed by a circle of dark palms, a strange building came into view. This crude construction, appearing as if it were cut from a single massive tree, looked like a giant chicken leg stabbed into the earth. Its trunk supported a crude, wooden platform. Steps, cut into the base, led up to a raised floor. At the centre of the makeshift platform, shaded by a rough sheet of corrugated tin, a blackened copper cauldron steamed over an open fire.

Reaching the crest of the hill, Corran walked into the shadow of the structure. Clumps of dense bamboo and barbed creepers that surrounded the perimeter of the tower formed a natural barrier. He found a gap in the leaves. As he slid through the narrow opening, thin tendrils, like needy fingers, reached out and pulled back on his ankles and shins. Fighting his way through the wall of foliage, he reached the base of the steps and paused to catch his breath. It had only been a modest walk up the hill, but Corran, sweating profusely, felt unusually drained. Wiping the moisture from his face, he paused before starting up the fragile steps that wound up and around the column of the trunk. They looked strong enough and it wasn't far, yet every slight movement, every tread seemed to require an inordinate effort. A climb that would normally have been counted in seconds appeared to take an eternity. It wasn't just tired, reluctant limbs that he was dragging up every inch of those unsteady, weak timbers; wiser, weaker versions of himself were already way down the hill, their joy to be away from the place echoing out like the last catchy refrain of a soft drinks commercial, sapping him of will and courage.

Eventually Corran made it to the top. The timbers of the platform, loose, without nails or ropes to secure them, shifted and groaned under his weight. One plank was so eaten by termites, it sank like a sponge under his foot, close to breaking. Instinctively, his arm reached to the floor for balance, making the structure shift precariously to the side. Although the whole fragile edifice was at least twelve feet off the ground it was a hasty construction; there were no railings or barriers to prevent anyone or anything falling over the edge.

Cutting blocks, sacking and blackened cooking utensils littered the rough floor. And at the centre of this dismal space, a dense pall of smoke swirled over the ominous copper cauldron.

Cautiously stepping over the unwashed cutlery and pots, Corran inched closer to the edge of the vessel. A rusting, battered lid, as if cut and hammered from the bonnet of a truck, hid whatever was softly simmering inside. As he bent forward to lift the edge of the cover, he was filled with trepidation,; a fleeting premonition that whatever was concealed inside would be horrific. But although this vision sickened him, the power of the aromas emanating from the steam (now undiluted by the wind), were so powerful and seductive, that it more than soothed his nerves. With a greasy cloth wrapped around his fingers as protection from the heat, he lifted the lid away and peered into the grim interior. The steam cleared to reveal a thick, boiling broth. At first there was nothing that remarkable or unusual about the stew – he could identify elements of lemon grass, star anise, perhaps fennel seeds, swimming within the sauces. But gradually, like something elementaly and repulsive emerging from a primordial gruel, three ghastly apparitions floated up from the depths. Half shrouded by the steam, the bloated, pallid, fleshy faces of Dao, Chin and Bao stared out, eyes dull and cloudy, a stream of hissing bubbles emanating from their nostrils and open mouths.

The lid dropped. Corran staggered back from the rim of the cauldron. Shot through with fear and dread, thoughts only of escape panicked his thinking. Instinctively his arm reached out to the column at the base of the steps to steady his legs. But then a second, more twisted imperative struggled in from his basest depths.

Curiosity is a mixed virtue. Left to roam freely it drives discovery; a wandering brook becomes a small tributary, its flow a great river. But often, when such emotions push us too far – often against our better interests – that urge to pry, rather than being silenced, becomes more forceful. From children's fairy stories to Hollywood horror, there is always a crucial boundary – the forbidden door, a secret box, the darker path unexplored. A similar irrepressible force propelled Corran back to the edge of the cauldron, he had to know more.

Shaking with unease, Corran reached for a ladle that hung from a nail at the edge of the fire. Again he wrapped the cloth around his fingers and slid the metal lid across to one side. Hiding his eyes from the ghoulish faces bobbing up and down within the oily froth, he dipped his spoon in at the side and scooped up a mouthful of the sauce. It was hot. Blowing over the ladle to soften the heat, he lifted it to his mouth and tasted. At first he felt little; the horror of what he had just witnessed had so scrambled his thoughts that it took a while to realign his senses. Textures came first – something coarse and indelicate. Then gradually, beginning with a simple distant note – a perfectly balanced fusion of lime, chilli and tamarind – a surge of unimaginable sensations invaded. As the tastes assaulted his senses, he stood there stupefied. It was as if the paths of every meal he had ever eaten, every dish, every spoon, every morsel, converged at this single point in time, a vision of the sublime. After four circumnavigations of the world and sixty-four countries, his quest had ended.

Greedy for more, Corran's attention returned to the cauldron. Now blind to the macabre spectacle at its core, he edged his spoon into the sauce for another, larger mouthful. Taking time to savour the flavours, a further barrage of deeper, more profound tastes overwhelmed him. So intense was this focus that all those previously hidden physiological functions – heart, valves and veins – appeared to pulse so faintly as to effectively freeze. His breath came in gulps, as if his lungs needed to be reminded to inflate and deflate.

Rising from the valley, the wind picked up. Leaves rustled. A wind chime sounded. It was close by, maybe at the edge of the platform. He paid no attention. Only the muffled groan of a floorboard finally stalled him: there was someone behind. With the ladle still raised to his mouth, he turned and saw the girl.

Few faces can corrupt a mind so completely. There were obvious dangers: a long, bloodied blade raised in her arms above him – yet Corran, focused only on her extraordinary beauty, remained dumbly paralysed, letting the last spoon of sauce dribble unchecked down his chin, like a child in a highchair.

Again it was the intensity of her eyes that he was so hopelessly drawn to. As she stood there unmoving, a last shaft of sunlight played over her face, highlighting the irresistible glow of her irises. It was as if he were looking directly through these lenses, seeing through several buried layers, each depth revealing darker, more turbulent histories and emotions – rage and fear fused with sadness and despair. It was here, locked inside the seething restless furnace of her past, that he read her signature – a recipe etched with revenge.

Thirty Eight

Corran could not recall whether the blade actually fell. If it had, there was no perceptible change in the girl's expression. Her eyes, the edges of her mouth, all remained cold, impassive, enigmatic.

Darkness folded over him. Following the fate of Dao, Chin and Bao, he felt himself sinking within the same seething, restless quagmire. Like so many other innocent victims – cows, pigs, chickens and ducks – he had so mercilessly despatched to the stews, soups and goulashes of his modest career, he saw himself in his turn, quietly simmering and softening within the luxuriant juices.

Hours later, the incessant pain of mosquito bites hauled him back to reality with an uncomfortable jolt. The temperature had turned; he felt as cold as an ice cube. Dew covered his face. He sat up on his elbows. Condensation, rolling down his forehead, found the sides of his mouth. Tasting the cool water brought on a wave of euphoria more eloquent than the rarest, most celebrated Beaujolais.

Reassured he was still living, Corran slowly took in his surroundings. He was lying in the dirt at the base of the platform. Looking up, he could see the night sky through the shattered floor timbers. A fall from such a height should have been enough to break his neck, yet he had survived. Reaching around the base of his skull, he felt something sticky and congealed that had fused with the strands of his hair. He panicked, thinking it was his splattered brains. It turned out to be crushed jack-fruit. Soft and over-ripe, its pulpy flesh had been the natural airbag that had cushioned his fall.

Weak and disoriented, Corran lifted himself up from the floor. In the gloom he could make out the edge of the blackened cauldron. Having fallen with him from the stage, it must have bounced off the ground, then come to rest in long reeds at the edge of the clearing. It was empty, its gruesome contents thankfully out of sight somewhere down the bank. Embers from the fire, strewn over the earth, glowed in the half-light.

Around the base of the central trunk, timbers from the rotten floor lay scattered in the dirt. Within these splinters he saw his mobile phone. The screen had shattered; it had probably been thrown from his pocket when he fell. Next to it, a long, thin shadow stretched out across the dusty floor. At the end of this dark line, something metallic glinted in the cold blue moonlight. Shuffling closer, Corran found the shaft of the kitchen knife. The long steel blade had lodged deep in the earth. It must have fallen harmlessly from her hands.

Thirty Nine

In front of the empty lakeside restaurant the lake was still. Bats skimmed low over the glass-like surface. A thin trail of bubbles rose from the depths.

Forty

Malee caught a songthaew to Khon Kaen and sat in a coffee shop near the bus station. It would be a short wait before catching the night express to Bangkok.

She had money; the police captain's wallet contained enough notes – sufficient for a cheap hotel until she could find a small place to stay.

Her aunt (a distant one at best) worked in a restaurant near a pier on the river. It was well known. Plenty of foreigners ate there. She was sure to find work.

It was just past midnight when Malee, comfortably curled up on the bench, was shaken awake. She sat up, blurry-eyed and dazed. Uniformed men surrounded her. A man with a peaked cap was bending over her.

"Where are you going?" he asked.

Malee, seeing the circle of officials, froze.

"Bangkok?" she muttered.

"You'd better hurry," the man said, nodding in the direction of a coach standing in a distant corner of the station, lit up by harsh fluorescent tube lights. "It's going in five minutes."

Dawn saw Malee wake a second time at the bus terminal at Mo

Chit, north of the capital. A short ride on the Skytrain took her to the Sathorn Pier. From there she caught a river boat to the Rama 8 Bridge. Aunt Sidar's restaurant was in Soi 5, minutes from the water.

At first the old woman didn't recognise Malee, let alone know who she was. Even the connecting relatives were tenuous, too distant for her memory.

"Boonthong, who's Boonthong, I don't know any Boonthongs" she muttered and complained.

Not that the memory lapse troubled her. At her age, now seventy-nine, she acknowledged that her recall wasn't as sharp as it used to be. Besides, Malee, if the girl really was related (as she was sure she was – such rare beauty could only have come by the Sapanpong line), had come to her at an opportune moment.

It wasn't just Aunt Sidar who ran restaurants – most of her family were involved with food; her sister had two noodle shops, an uncle a bar, grandparents a cake shop. Her godson rented out food stalls at the weekend market. But more importantly, on that day, at that very moment, her eldest son was opening his first venue, a Manhattan-style brasserie close to Silom, she was going there now.

One hundred and fifty guests had been invited. Florentine steaks were the highlight of the evening. Four cow carcasses, grass-fed dry aged beef, had been delivered from Galloway, Australia. But for two hours they had blocked the double doors of the walk-in fridge freezer because no one had the butcher's skills to quarter the meat.

Aunt Sidar, furious at such a fundamental oversight, berated the manager. Looking crushed, overwhelmed, the man was on the verge of walking out, when Malee, stepping forward from the back of the room, offered her services.

Initially sceptical that the young girl would be up to the job – she was young, too thin, they'd only known her ten minutes – the staff were nevertheless impressed when she produced her own knives. They were tightly wrapped in a rough canvas pouch she kept in her knapsack. Beautifully clean, they were razor sharp. Malee selected a small five-inch boning blade to make the first incisions.

Astonished by the girl's virtuosity, a quiet came over the kitchen. Unlike brawny butchers that shattered bone from joint with coarse swinging hacks, Malee made delicate, precise incisions, her dexterity revealing a mastery and control that for the younger ones, gawping open-mouthed at her uncanny familiarity with the intricacies of mammal anatomy (bone, sinews and muscles) – was close to sensual. Soon precisely-cut chunks of tender red meat – sirloin, porterhouse, T-bone, ribeye, neck and brisket – were neatly lined up on the chopping block.

Aunt Sidar's son Panna, drawn inside by the unexpected lull of activity in the kitchen, caught the tail end of the performance. He called her "beauty with a blade". The term stuck, as did the restaurant's enviable reputation for serving up the best steaks in town. A year later, his establishment a success, Panna changed the title of the restaurant to this nickname.

Epilogue

The Story of Food, Corran's troublesome opus, never hit the printing presses. The litigation, as Amy had long indicated, was painful. Andresen and Favia (for she was now joint CEO), having fully absorbed his former publisher, Font Lescari, into their media empire, had been unforgiving. The New York attorney firm, Kirkland, Blackrock, Bowles, described by *Forbes* Magazine as the law firm 'most likely to strike dread' into the hearts of the prosecuted, were engaged. More than big guns, they were a Blitzkrieg to slay minnows. To show some contrition and to speed a settlement, Corran admitted all guilt and culpability. It wasn't enough. They wanted pain. In keeping with its global reach, Font Lescari sought costs and damages across three continents – an unnecessary complication that multiplied the defence costs and produced a deluge of paperwork.

Corran's five restaurants were closed and his businesses wound up. Over the coming months his phone fell silent and his emails dried up. Corran's once august position in the league of top chefs slumped by the day and sunk below the waterline. By the end of the lawsuit, his fame and reputation had evaporated, his old life washed away.

As the final packing cases were removed from his Sydney harbour offices, the post delivered one last letter – a postcard from Amy. She was successful, married, happy with two children, houses in Florida and Connecticut and two dogs.

Corran moved to San Diego on the west coast of the States. After a month in a Holiday Inn on the seafront, he found a small room in a motel – two fifties-style blocks with balconies folded around a kidney-shaped pool. For money Corran took a job as a tennis coach at a sports club in Mission Valley, training kids, families, old people and the retired. It was part-time work, mostly afternoons when the sun was low and the coaching more ball-boy than tennis pro. Undemanding, yes, but it didn't expose his shortcomings as a player who hadn't really seen a court for five years.

The walk back up the hill to his City Heights motel skirted the park and the zoo. He often stopped by at the local convenience store to pick up a meal – cheese enchiladas, tinned ravioli or prepackaged macaroni, fast in the microwave.

It was a long time before he could bring himself to eat flesh again. Anything resembling a stew or a thick meaty sauce turned his stomach. Mostly it was burgers, at their most sanitised, processed and frozen. BeefBox, Best Burger and Square Deal fitted the profile of the perfectly mechanised meal. He ate alone, watched box-sets and Latin American TV novelas and swam late at night when the pool was empty and unlit.

As bland and empty as his existence had become, he found his life adrift not entirely without purpose. It was a six-mile walk down the beach from his apartment to the tennis club. Nobody knew him or spoke to him. As a stranger he had time to forget, to think, to plan. As his pain and lethargy eased, a restlessness returned.

By late summer he'd saved enough to travel. He took a taxi to the airport with no fixed ideas, intent or itinerary. Hopping atolls across the Pacific, from Hawaii to Tahiti and Fuji, he found himself by chance back in Tokyo and the port front of Shijomae. New apartments and a promenade had replaced the seaweed-strewn beach where he had washed up two years before. Surprisingly, the Hiro San had survived the onslaught of the developers. Corran's attack (for that was how it had been reported in the press), had made Mori, more than a local hero, a national hero. The outpouring of sympathy on TV and the press had brought him some fame – a defender of the nation's traditions and heritage against the avarice of foreign invaders. Cast in such a glowing populist light, the developers hadn't dared confront the silver-haired 'hero'. Abandoning their ambitious plans, the construction company went back to the drawing board. Mori was invited onto the advisory board as a 'cultural consultant'. Rather than pulling down the old timber buildings, the developers had them carefully restored and preserved.

Corran, trying to get a close look at the table where he had last dined with Jade, was recognised by a waiter; few guests had provided such high drama and amusement. Old Mori himself came out to celebrate his return. A rare sake was brought out, Biwa No Choju, made with organic rice in paddies where carp bred. Despite the long interlude, Corran was shown to a table to experience the courses he had failed to finish. The dessert, the renowned sake and juniper snowflakes, reputably Mori's finest, was well worth the wait.

The Hiro San, Mori patiently explained, never had a secret formula. And Corran hadn't been the first to try his luck and sneak into their kitchen. The shrine was exactly that. A shrine to the ancestors. Not even his ancestors. His family couldn't even boil an egg. Mori himself had been an insurance salesman in a previous life. And not a very good one. He had used an inheritance from an uncle in Osaka to take over the Hiro San in the late eighties. The original owners were only too happy to abandon their failing, crumbling enterprise and retreat to a modern retirement village in the suburbs of Gunwa close to a golf course and spa. Since then it had taken Mori thirty years to master his art.

Corran took a small bedsit in a side street close to the port. On quiet days Mori graciously allowed him into the kitchen. He was given a low stool in the corner from where he could watch the chefs. After a month he was still there. Mori, noticing his restlessness, allowed him to help out. A long way from the actual cooking, he was given small menial tasks – cleaning, preparation, grinding and slicing. Inching up the skills chain, Corran was told to forget all his past. That was easy; his restaurants, books and recipes had all gone. Despite his obeisance, it took Corran a year to be fully accepted as part of the inner family.

In the autumn Mori went into the mountains; a foraging expedition for mushrooms and roots. He usually went alone. Corran asked to go with him. Packing lunch boxes and backpacks, they took the old Eizan line to Kurama and hiked into the valley to the small hamlet of Hanase. Their accommodation was higher still; a small hunting lodge deep in the cedar woods of the Kitayama mountains.

With thick grey cloud shrouding both the valley and the high peaks, Corran found the forest grim and oppressive. The tall dark pines that surrounded the modest hut, undoubtedly majestic, hemmed in the view like the bars of a prison. The damp irritated his chest. He slept badly. At night it was bitterly cold. There weren't enough blankets (Mori, knowing what to expect had cunningly raided the store cupboard). The insects, a biting centipede and the mukade hornets, were intrepid and hostile.

Given time, his list of complaints eased. Sitting on the steps of the porch, he watched the mist roll up the valley through the trees. Silver streams of water wandered between gnarled roots and rocks. The fierce, incessant rain had a certain rhythm – there were soothing interludes, messages whispered between distant valleys.

For two days, nothing happened. They chewed Anpan, sweet rolls filled with black sesame and red bean paste, brewed tea and listened to the rain fall. Mori didn't talk to Corran, no idle comments, instruction or questions were exchanged between them.

Not that the old man was silent. For most of the day he chatted aimlessly like a teenager locked to a cellphone. Most of this conversation was directed to plants, a wandering insect and, when he got the chance, animals. Although morsels of sugary food were obviously the key factor in attracting the wildlife in the first place, Mori did appear to make a genuine connection with them and build some elemental rapport. Late in the afternoon there was often an impressive menagerie outside his balcony – a pair of grey squirrels, a pine marten, a young Sika deer. Rarest of all, a shy Serow, an animal closely related to a wild goat even ate from his hand.

Corran was woken early on the third day by the sound of movement in the back of the hut. At first he thought a black bear might have broken into the kitchen to steal their rolls – it was Mori preparing his backpack. Corran pulled back the curtains thinking that a break in the clouds might have prompted his actions. He was wrong. The weather hadn't changed. If anything it was bleaker, the rain heavier, falling in sheets.

Carrying wicker baskets, they set off up the mountainside. Crossing a steep ravine, the track narrowed and became steeper. Corran, losing his grip on the slippery scree, found a short willow branch in the undergrowth for use as a climbing stick.

By mid-morning they had climbed a considerable distance and height. Corran had concerns, they'd packed water but no food. Mori, brushing off such parochial anxieties, laughed. The forest was his natural pantry. On both sides of the winding track, he pointed to the low branches of a tree or bush; there were still late juniper berries, roots and wild herbs, the flavours sharp and astringent.

Mori, attuned to this primal environment – the trees, ferns, herbs and mosses – was knowledgable. Removed of brash nutritional labelling, tastes, textures and smells were his guide. For foragers and those that lived off the mountain, such knowledge was critical; a narrow divide separated pleasure and pain, health and sickness and, at extremes, life and death.

In the first century AD, an ancient Ayurvedic text described the struggles of the wisest sages of the land to document how many tastes existed in the universe. From impossibly large numbers, a list was reduced to four. Four tastes that aligned with the cosmological elements of earth, fire, water and wind. Though this list didn't satisfy all. One *rishi* countered with two: those that brought life and those that took it away.

The first mushrooms appeared suddenly. Maybe their growth was tied to high altitude? In the shadow of trees, bushes and rocks,

Mori pointed out the edible from those best left alone. There were the popular *shiitake*, clumps of mattock, often grilled with tempura, the *enoki* eaten mainly for its texture, *kirurage* and the dumpy, glossy wood jellyfish used in salads.

But it wasn't a simple free-for-all buffet. The mysterious and delicate angel wings, recognisable by their distinctive, fluted underside, were so popular, they had filled the shelves of city supermarkets. But then something had changed in the environment – maybe plants nearby or nutrients in the soil: the mushrooms had become toxic and people had died.

The holy grail of fungi-hunting in Japan was the *matsutake*. With a distinctive spicy scent, described by early Japanese writers as embodying an 'autumn aroma', the mushroom was more sought after and valuable then European truffles – although profit was never ever a motive in Mori's design. Appearing at the onset of the October rains, *matsutake* were usually found hidden in leaf litter a short distance from the base of red cedars. Choosing only trees that are several decades old, the fine threads of their mycelial fibres have a symbiotic relationship with the tree roots – minerals and water are exchanged for glucose and sucrose. The mushrooms thrived in old woodlands used by traditional villages and farms. When forests became industrialised and used only for timber, the ancient woodlands were taken down. Only recently was that imbalance reversed, allowing the *matsutake* to return.

Never cut with a knife (steel tainted the flesh), only the largest were picked. Instead Mori used his fingers to separate the soil away from the base of the fungi, as they were gently encouraged out from their roots. The soft break made a distinctive tearing sound, like a rice cracker being shared. Mori, placing the mushrooms carefully in his wicker basket, wrapped them with *sawara* leaves to keep them fresh and unbruised.

Late in the afternoon, with baskets filled, they separated. Corran wanted to take a longer route, higher up, that provided a view of the adjoining valley, he had heard of a monastery to the north. Mori gave instructions, picked up the mushrooms and headed back down through the cedars in the direction of the shack.

Without the distraction of searching for food, Corran reached the summit quickly. But with the forest so densely packed, it was difficult finding a view through the trees, let alone a path. Deep gullies on the far side fell sharply, the serrated boulders on their edge, polished and slippery. It was getting late. He started downhill.

A thin track followed a stream that weaved between tall limestone boulders. Leaving the tall cedar woods behind, the path dropped into a dense bamboo thicket. Blown by the wind, the hollow stems cracked and groaned. Folded, compressed and abruptly snapping loose, they sounded like the echo of a thousand doors opening and slamming closed again.

A wrong turn brought him out on a rocky promontory above the gorge. He was still some way from the shack, its position marked by a thin trail of smoke from its kitchen fire, he imagined Mori warming his tea. Taking in the descent, he looked down on the dark feathers of a sparrow hawk gliding silently by.

Searching for a way down, Corran fell twice. A misjudged foot landed a boot in a stream. The chill water seeped through the outer fabric of the shoe to his toes. Scrambling back to the bank, brambles tore his trousers and cut through to his ankles. There was blood and it stung. Shutting out the pain, he wandered on through the damp undergrowth and rocks. As his mind drifted, a state of aimlessness opened up his senses to his surroundings. Small minutiae became his focus – a carpet of bronze, ochre and yellow; the first fallen leaves of autumn. Raindrops dripped through beards of damp lichen. Trailing his hand through the ferns, he felt the texture of wet leaves against his open palm and caught the scent of moss crushed beneath his step.

A weak ray of sunlight penetrated the haze. The low light, distorted by the thin rain, produced a halo effect; a spinning disc of luminous cloud that hovered, much like a giant Christmas tree star, above the tips of the pines. Corran recalled such an image in a book from his childhood; the prophet Ezekiel, grovelling on his knees, primed to receive a message from the Lord, blinded by its magnificence.

Revelation, wasn't that how every spiritual quest ended? It wouldn't take much to burn such a transcript into the swirling wisps of mist. But Corran, too hungry and blunt for such a calling, was pleased enough just for its warmth.

The brief tunnel of light illuminated a track that wound its way down into the valley. A rust-tinted quail hopped between the shinning pebbles. Surrendering himself to its guidance, he walked down.

Corran got back late. It was dark. Mori was just getting up after a sleep. A fire was lit. He uncovered the wicker basket of mushrooms and removed the *matsutake*. There was no recipe. He wiped the dried earth away with a damp cloth and grilled them over a hot stone.

Curtain of Rain
Tew Bunnag
224 pages
ISBN 978 616 7339 49 8

Two lives, fatefully interlinked; two sets of memories, in danger of being lost. Clare Stone's past has suddenly caught up with her. When a long-suppressed memory comes vividly alive, she finds herself being pulled back to the place of its origin: Bangkok. There, she meets Tarrin Wandee, the writer whose book has unsettled her. But have they met before, all those years ago, when she was young, idealistic and dangerously naïve?

All our lives are linked; it's just a question of how. Moody and atmospheric, *Curtain of Rain* is a story of politics, power and greed, and the search for meaning and redemption.

After the wave
Tew Bunnag
118 pages
ISBN 978 616 7339 59 7

Tew decided to write this collection of short stories linked to the Tsunami, inspired by his experiences of working in the South of Thailand with those who had suffered the devastation at first hand and were dealing with the loss of their families and friends, as well as, in some cases, their livelihoods, stories which touch on universal issues of loss, grief and recovery.

Siamese Tears (A novel)
The kingdom's struggle against the colonial superpowers
Claire Keefe-Fox
392 pages
ISBN 978 616 7339 75 7

Siam 1890 and blue-stocking Julie Gallet, an independent-minded Parisian, has made what her English mother describes as an imprudent match. Follow- ing her husband to the Far East, she comes to stay with Michael Crawfurd, her British diplomat cousin and discovers a city of golden spires and colonial intrigue between France and England. Resisting entreaties to return home, Julie settles in Bangkok, teaches French to the ladies of the Royal Court and be- comes passionately involved in Siamese life and affairs. Her irreverent journal recounts her growing political awareness along with the awakening of her sensuality. Blending fact and fiction, Siamese Tears is a faithful account of the events leading to the Paknam incident through the eyes of those who wit- nessed them.

A Woman of Angkor (A novel)
John Burgess
500 pages
ISBN 978 616 7339 25 2

In a village in 12th century Cambodia, birthplace of the lost Angkor civilisation, behind a towering stone temple, lives a young woman named Sray. Her neighbours liken her to the heroine of a Hindu epic, but her serenity is marred by a dangerous secret. One rainy season afternoon, she is called to a life of prominence in the royal court. There, her faith and loyalties will be tested by the great king Suryavarman II.

"Burgess has done something that I believe is unique in modern writing: set a credible and seemingly authentic tale in the courts and temples of ancient Angkor to stir the imagination and excite our historical interest." (John le Carré)

The Stairway Guide's Daughter
John Burgess
306 pages
ISBN 978 616 7339 87 0

In twelfth century Cambodia, a young woman called Jorani earns her living guiding pilgrims up a two thousand-step stairway to the magnificent cliff-top temple Preah Vihear. One day, she accidentally witnesses the furtive burning of sacred palm-leaf documents, and is drawn into a succession struggle at the temple. She is forced to choose between loyalty to family and to the son of the abbot, with whom she forms an unlikely bond. Set in the golden age of Cam-bodia's Angkor civilization, *The Stairway Guide's Daughter* brings to life a tem-ple that is one of humankind's most remarkable creations of faith and architecture, and is today a UNESCO World Heritage Site.

COMING SOON

The Blind Earthworm in the Labyrinth
Veeraporn Nitiprapha
Translated by Kong Rithdee